Controversies in Sociology
edited by
Professor T. B. Bottomore and Dr M. J. Mulkay

4

Dilemmas of Discourse

in the same series

Dilemmas
of Discourse

*Controversies about
the Sociological Interpretation
of Language*

by

ANTHONY WOOTTON

*Lecturer in Sociology
University of York*

Holmes & Meier Publishers
New York

First Published in the United States in 1976
by Holmes & Meier Publishers, Inc.
101 Fifth Avenue
New York, New York 10003

Library of Congress Cataloging in Publication Data

Wootton, Anthony J.
  Dilemmas of discourse.

  (Controversies in sociology; 4)
  Bibliography: p.
  Includes index
  1. Sociolinguistics. I. Title.
P40.W6   301.2'1   75-35651
ISBN 0-8419-0247-X

Printed in Great Britain

6

For Trespassers W and the rest

Preface

This book is intended to clarify some of the issues bound up with recent approaches and controversy concerning the way in which sociologists go about analysing talk. As the discussion proceeds it will become clear that I am not just presenting a dispassionate overview of these issues, but that for various reasons, which I try to make explicit, I favour certain lines of enquiry rather than others. I hope that this has not led me to misrepresent the views of protagonists in the debate and that the book is somewhat more provocative and lively as a result. My main intellectual debt which is not recognised in the text is to my colleague Paul Drew, who has helped me work out a great number of issues as a result of his reading the whole text. My wife, Seonaid, and the editors of the series have also helped eliminate the more overt stylistic and grammatical infelicities.

A*

Contents

1

Language, Concepts and Description

Sociology is intimately concerned with the study of what people say. Much time is spent in methodology courses discussing the ways in which what people say can be transformed into data, how the context in which a question is being asked influences a person's response, and so on. After some consideration of such issues it soon becomes clear that handling responses and deciding on the status they can be assigned is no easy matter. In fact it is rather complex, and by complex I think we usually mean that there are problems such as deciding whether a particular response counts as an instance of some analytic category (the coding problem); deciding whether the way in which a response is classified does justice to the point of view being expressed in the original response; or deciding on the most reliable way of classifying responses. Such problems are mainly addressed in the context of survey enquiry, but they are in fact even more acute in naturalistic enquiry. In the latter case, for example, there is less chance of some standard response elicitation technique, and much interpretation will be based on the analyst's implicit classification of conversations going on around him. On the other hand, the participant observer is generally held to be in a position to pick up the meanings and nuances of what is going on around him, so that the looseness in the handling of data is compensated for by greater validity.

Most of the early argument in this first chapter will be concerned with how we as sociologists deal with what people say in naturally occurring situations. I shall be trying to indicate what seem to me some less frequently acknowledged problems associated with handling such talk, and the alternative approaches to such problems which seem to be available and which constitute the major controversy to which this book is addressed. Briefly stated, the controversy centres around the question of whether it is more accurate and useful to determine the meaning of what we say independently of the particular context in which it is said. If, for example, someone says, 'I promise you that I'll do it for you', does it make more sense to think of such promises as having some distinctive meaning by virtue of the words 'I promise . . .', or does it make more sense to think of the meaning of an utterance beginning 'I promise . . .' as always being an occasioned meaning, in the sense of always being a product of the specific circumstances in which it is uttered?

Posed in this way the argument looks fairly innocuous, but it is one which, though rarely presented in this form, has led to some controversy within sociology because it represents, as I understand it, the heart of the issue which divides ethnomethodologists from conventional sociologists. It is rarely presented in this way, I think, for two main reasons. First, many critics of ethnomethodology are simply misinformed as to the nature of the intellectual issues at stake, misinformed in part because of the notorious stylistic difficulties in ethnomethodolgical writing. The second reason is tied up with the tendency to associate phenomenological writing such as that of Schutz with ethnomethodological writing, so that debate has revolved around more abstract notions of meaning rather than meaning and language. This tendency is understandable in that the intellectual development of Garfinkel, the founding father of ethnomethodology, was bound up with attempts to accommodate some of the writing of Schutz, among others (see Garfinkel, 1967, Chapter 8). In this book it is argued that the distinctive stance of ethnomethodology is founded on a particular view of the relation between language and meaning, one which in many ways bears comparison with the view of language which is developed in some of Wittgenstein's later writings. An adequate critique of this stance, therefore, will have to concern itself with demonstrating that this view of the relation between language and meaning is inadequate in some way, and I shall try to give some idea of the lines along which such an alternative position would need to be established and the kinds of loopholes which it leaves undefended. This occupies most of Chapters 2 and 3.

In this chapter I want to begin by giving a preliminary idea of the two views of language being discussed by tracing them out in connection with a sociological study which is naturalistic in flavour. The issue is approached in this way because in most sociological inquiry of this kind the distinctions I am going to make are concealed and ambiguous, so that there is no clearcut school of thought in sociology which can be said to have categorically represented one view rather than the other in the past. The work I want to discuss is a paper on 'normal crimes' written by Sudnow (1965), and I choose this paper because it represents in a number of ways a typical sociological strategy for coming to grips with talk.[1]

Sudnow's argument is developed in the context of research which he carried out in a metropolitan area of an American city. He was interested in the way in which plea bargaining took place between the District Attorney (DA), Public Defender (PD)[2] and those accused of having committed some crime (clients of the PD). His argument is that decisions concerning the type of plea a client makes depend heavily on the PD and DA's conception of whether the case is typical of its class – whether it is a normal burglary or child molestation, for example. If the case is typical of its class, a typical form of reduced plea will be entered on behalf of the client, although this has to be negotiated with the client beforehand by the PD. Typical burglaries are in this way reduced to petty theft if the client agrees to plead guilty, typical child molestation to loitering around a schoolyard, and so on. So far, then, the framework is a recognisably sociological one; PDs and DAs hold some notion of normal crimes. In traditional sociology this would be described as a role conception; in more Schutzian terminology, a typification. These conceptions, the argument implies, are applied by PDs and DAs to clients who come before them; and deciding whether a conception is warranted in any specific case requires the official to look for *indications* that the case is a normal one of its type. Thus according to Sudnow (1965, p. 260), normal burglaries would involve regular violators, no weapons, low-priced items, little property damage, lower class establishments, largely Negro defendants and a non-professional orientation to crime. In the case of child molestation, loitering would be an important indication of normality.

From the range of evidence and information which Sudnow presents, there seems little doubt that the PD and DA in this situation do hold some notion of 'normal crimes', together with sets of typical indications, and that such notions play a significant part in their dealings with clients. To illustrate this, Sudnow provides us with some examples of first interviews between PDs and their clients, interviews in which the PD had no information about the defendant and the particular crime other than the client's record (taken at the beginning of the interview), and that provided by the penal code number which gives the nature of the original charge brought against the client. In the example reproduced below the charge was child molestation.

> *PD:* OK why don't you start out by telling me how this thing got started?
> *Defendant:* Well, I was at the park and all I did was to ask this little girl if she wanted to sit on my lap for awhile and you know, just sit on my lap. Well, about twenty minutes later I'm walkin down the street about a block away from the park and this cop pulls up and there the same little girl is, you know, sitting in the back seat with the same dame. The cop asks me to stick my head in the back seat and he asks the kid if I was the one and she says yes. So he puts me in the car and takes a statement from me and here I am in the joint. All I was doin was playin with her a little . . .
> *PD (interrupting):* . . . OK I get the story, let's see what we can do. If I can get this charge reduced to a misdemeanour then I would advise you to plead guilty, particularly since you have a record and that wouldn't look too well in court with a jury.
> (the interview proceeded for another 2 or 3 minutes and the decision to plead guilty was made)

Sudnow's claim here is that

> . . . the PD interrupted when he had enough information to con-
> firm his sense of the case's typicality and construct a typifying
> portrayal of the present defendant.
> [ibid., p. 268]

Again it is important to stress that Sudnow's claim is not remark-able. It is the sort of claim that warrants our use of the ideas of role conception and typification; and if these ideas are not applicable to real life encounters in some way such as this, one must surely begin to question their relevance and utility for the study of social phenomena.

I want to deal first with Sudnow's claim as to what is going on in this stretch of talk. In effect he is providing us with a formulation which it is possible for him to make given his knowledge of the context and the sorts of purposes he knows that the PD has in this sort of situation. The adequacy of Sudnow's claims in this case must rest on his formulation being the correct or, less strongly, the most likely formulation of the occasion. Given that we do not have a direct statement from the PD himself about this matter, however, a number of other formulations might well suggest themselves as alternatives to the one provided by Sudnow. Two of them are presented below.

1   The PD had decided beforehand that, in the light of his clients' record, he would recommend him to plead guilty to some lesser offence; that the interview from the PD's point of view was a burdensome necessity; and that the main aim was to ascertain whether the client would be reasonable enough to go along with his decision. One could hold, therefore, that the typification of 'reasonable client' was the one most relevant to the interaction from the PD's point of view.

2   The PD was not concerned with classifying his client at all, but with making some preliminary assessment of whether there were any likely grounds which might warrant a plea of not guilty. For various reasons, such as the time at his disposal, his own incompetence, and the status of his client, this assessment was handled in a trivial, perfunctory manner, but nevertheless this constituted the relevant framework within which the PD saw the interaction.

We, as sociologists, are confronted with the problem of having to decide which of these three formulations is the most adequate; though it should of course be noted that the problem of adequacy is not confronted only by sociologists. It is a matter which is also routinely confronted in one form or another by most people in society, most explicitly by such groups as lawyers, social workers and psychiatrists. Sudnow, of course, might argue that his formulation is the most adequate on the grounds that from his knowledge of what regularly happens in this context this seems, on the basis of his experience, the most likely interpretation. This, however, does not resolve the issue. First, it stands in danger of becoming tautological. If the example is used as evidence of a wider pattern, but cannot be explicated without assuming the existence of that wider pattern, the argument becomes precarious. Second, and more important, even if we grant that a wider pattern exists, that PDs and DAs for example hold some notion of 'normal crimes', it can always be made problematic whether, *in this instance*, that notion is being employed. There are rules in our society concerning the nature of contracts, norms regarding marital fidelity, ethical practices relating to the behaviour of doctors, but it really does not make sense to say that the sheer existence of such conventions resolves, in any specific case, doubts as to whether these conventions are being observed. Similarly, in our own example, the appeal to wider conventions does not help us resolve the problem of the alternative formulations provided for the talk.

Suppose for the moment that during the interview with his client the PD had said something like, 'Well, your case seems to be typical of a number of other cases concerning young children and I have found that the best way to handle the matter . . .' Would this then allow us to draw the inference which Sudnow draws, that the PD stopped gathering information when he had assessed whether the case was an instance of normal child molesting? One could still argue, however, that what the PD meant was ambiguous in that it does not definitively exclude the alternative formulations as to what was happening, which I provided earlier. In connection with either of these interpretations it could be argued, for example, that the PD's statement was an attempt to 'cool out' the client, a well-known strategy for dealing with this kind of person in this kind of situation (see Goffman, 1962).

In dealing with the talk in this way I am raising some analytic issues concerning the way we as sociologists relate concepts to verbal labels which represent these concepts, and to indications which warrant the use of a verbal label. I have agreed, and this needs emphasising, that PDs may hold some notion of 'normal crime', but whether they hold it in any instance is only accessible to us via their talk, as we have no access to their minds, so in any instance we have to decide whether the talk indicates the operation of such a concept/typification. In this case we have to decide whether the PD's claim that this is a typical child molestation is a *genuine* descriptive statement and not a snub or an attempt to cool someone out. If we can provide a set of rules which will allow us to make such distinctions as analysts, then clearly we will be approaching Sudnow's goal of providing an unambiguous formulation of what is going on in this stretch of talk.

Another way in which such an unambiguous reading might be facilitated would centre around the relation of the words 'typical child molestation' to the indications which warrant the use of the phrase. I have already mentioned that, according to Sudnow, loitering is taken as an indication of normal child molestation, no weapons and so on as an indication of a normal burglary. If we could establish that a phrase such as 'typical child molestation' is tied to the occurrence of specific indications such as these, that the use of the phrase is governed by the presence or absence of such indications, then we would be in the position of being able to specify the meanings of the words and phrases being used in a more un-ambiguous fashion. We would be able to say, for example, that as the PD refers to the case as a typical child molestation, this means that certain features are present, such as loitering. If the meanings of the phrases and words which we use are not usefully subject to this kind of analysis, if for example the indications which warrant the use of phrases such as 'typical child molestation' are funda-mentally ambiguous in some way, then this clearly also has implica-tions for our ability as analysts to provide adequate unequivocal formulations of what is going on in any stretch of talk.

Hence, if our aim is to provide an adequate reading, formulation or description for a stretch of talk, the extent to which this is a fruitful analytic exercise will depend on whether we can extract unambiguously one formulation rather than a set of alternative formulations, and whether *this* is possible will depend on whether it is feasible to develop general criteria for deciding the meaning of words and general criteria for deciding what sort of utterance an utterance is. The viabilily of such an enterprise therefore rests on some assumptions about the nature of language, and it is because they take a different view of the nature of language that the ethnomethodologists reject the viability of such an approach. For the ethnomethodologists, words are essentially indexical[3] expres-sions; expressions whose meaning relies on the context in which they are used in such a way that attempts to delineate the meaning of words in some more general way are both misleading and in-complete. For them, the more relevant strategy is not the extraction of an incorrigible reading or formulation; it is the exploration of *how* one makes sense of utterances which are in effect bundles of indexical expressions. Many sociologists and linguists, however, would want to defend the view that the meaning of words and utterances is not *that* ambiguous, and that in some sense it is possible to devise general criteria for deciding the meaning of words in such a way as to allow us to achieve the kind of formulation which is the aim of Sudnow's analysis.

One possible misunderstanding of the ethnomethodological position is worth mentioning. Because the utterances we use are indexical expressions whose *precise* meaning in any strict sense is glossed over, this does not mean that, when people speak, they themselves feel terribly unsure of what they are talking about. This is not an implication of the ethnomethodological approach, although it would be an implication of their approach that the way in which glossing avoids the specification of precise meanings leads to a

range of typical ways in which other people's remarks can be undercut by such techniques as doubting, criticising and finding fault (see
Garfinkel and Sacks, 1970). These points can again be illustrated
in the context of Sudnow's example. The question which ethnomethodologists find most interesting in connection with such talk
is that of deciding how it is that we come to read or formulate the
talk in a particular way, or how it is that we can arrive at a reading
similar to that of Sudnow. They are not claiming that when Sudnow
heard the conversation it was fundamentally ambiguous to him;
if it had been ambiguous, presumably he would not have provided
us with the formulation which he did. Nevertheless the words and
utterances in the talk can be taken as ambiguous. I have traded on
this ambiguity in suggesting that a statement such as, 'If I can get
this charge reduced to a misdemeanour then I would advise you to
plead guilty' can be treated in a number of different ways, for
example as advice, or as an attempt to cool out, or as a warning.
The ethnomethodologist's strategy, then, is to explore how it is
possible to hear this statement as cooling out, if it is heard in that
way, and to explore the methods by which such ambiguities are
resolved by hearers. An alternative view might suggest that one *can*
arrive at an adequate description of what is happening here by
deciding on a relatively unambiguous formulation of the talk.
Whether such a position is viable depends, I have argued, on the
extent to which it is possible to treat the meanings of words, utterances and expressions as having definable properties.

Clearly the issues which are being raised here are not peculiarly
sociological issues. Problems surrounding the notion of meaning
have been perennial ones in both philosophy and linguistics, and
I want now to give some preliminary and simplified idea of the way
in which such issues are tackled within these different bodies of
knowledge.

So far I have been partly concerned with examining connections
between concepts which people hold, such as 'normal child molestation', and actual instances of talk. Many linguists, however, would
be chary of letting *concepts* play such a prominent part in their
investigations. Householder writes:

If we are not to be caught in an infinite regress, we cannot suppose
that speaking is a kind of translation (as is often done); we think
some profound thought (in an unknown form) and then 'code'
it or translate it from the unknown form into English. If this were
so, then it is difficult to imagine what the underlying form of

thought could be but another language – one, alas, inaccessible
to study, but about which we could ask again how thoughts are
put into this form.
[1971, p. 22, quoted in Coulter, 1973]

Lyons (1968, Chapter 9) also argues that an approach emphasising
the concepts lying behind language encourages subjectivism and
introspection, and that the linguistic investigation of meaning should
proceed empirically and as independently as possible from philosophical disputes concerning such matters as the status of concepts.
Up to 1960, however, the investigation of semantics by linguists
was of relatively minor significance in the overall development of
linguistic theory. Bloomfield, for example, simply used native informants' judgements concerning the similarity between words as
his primary data from which units at various levels of investigation
(such as phonemes and morphemes) could be discovered by explicit
analytic procedures. Semantics was discussed, but the definition of
meaning used by Bloomfield was so wide that the systematic inte-
gration of semantic description with other types of linguistic description seemed a fruitless task. Bloomfield writes:

We have defined the meaning of a linguistic form as the situation
in which the speaker utters it and the response which it calls
forth in the hearer . . . The situations which prompt people to
utter speech include every object and happening in their universe.
In order to give a scientifically accurate definition of meaning for
every form of a language, we should have to have a scientifically
accurate knowledge of everything in the speaker's world.
[1933, p. 139]

While Chomsky's writings (1957, 1965) radically changed linguistic
procedures for describing grammars, their continuity with previous
work in the realm of semantics is perhaps most striking, and it was
not until Fodor and Katz's work that a systemmatic attempt was
made to make semantics a part of linguistic description. Their work
(1964) was essentially developed in connection with the new approach to linguistic description begun by Chomsky, and it does not
purport to be a complete theory of meaning in the sense intended
by Bloomfield. A crucial part of their enterprise is an attempt to
extract the primary or dictionary meaning of words, and they try
to achieve this by distinguishing the primary dimensions along
which a word contrasts with other vocabulary items. This concern

for dimensions of contrast is an important structuralist assumption underlying modern linguistics – an assumption deriving from Saussure (1916), who stressed how the value of any linguistic item derives from the relations which that item contracts with other items within a given system. In practice, this means that instead of focussing on the *reference* of words, what words stand for in the outside world, the emphasis is on the sense of words,[4] the ways in which they contrast with other vocabulary items, on features like synonymy (sameness of meaning), antonymy (oppositeness of meaning) and hyponymy (the extent to which the meaning of some words can be said to be included in those of others, for example 'scarlet' in 'red'). For Fodor and Katz, the semantic markers relevant to the to the sense discriminations of the word 'bachelor' would be (Human) and (Animal) and (Male), with (Male) appearing along two paths, one that connects with the distinguisher ('Who has never married') and one that connects with the distinguisher ('Young fur seal without a mate').[5] This is necessary in order to distinguish two conventional senses of 'bachelor'; first, an unmarried male; second, a young fur seal.

Again it should be emphasised that, in setting up these formulations, linguists are not attempting to model the total knowledge which speakers are employing when using these expressions, or the full meaning which is conveyed by the use of some item. For this reason these kinds of semantic analysis usually make strong assumptions as to the absence of contextual interference on the meaning of an item, assumptions which I shall try to make more explicit in Chapter 2. Furthermore the point of making such sense discriminations of words is tied very closely in linguistics to the debate about whether semantic distinctions such as these are necessary for an adequate grammatical description of a language and, if so, of deciding in what sense and in what ways the syntactic rules which generate sentences are dependent on semantic elements. The adequacy of such an enterprise as Fodor and Katz's, therefore, is to be assessed in linguistic terms according to whether the framework they devise radically improves the power of linguistic rules to generate acceptable sentences.[6]

Implicit in the work of Fodor and Katz is the sharp and typical linguistic distinction between competence and performance. Most linguists have always wanted to take as their primary unit of analysis a language, and as their primary data a set of statements which are linguistically acceptable in a specific linguistic community. Their concern has been to construct a set of rules which account for the form which these linguistically acceptable statements take, so that in Chomsky's terms writing a grammar is a similar enterprise to that of constructing a theory which accounts for a set of phenomena. Fodor and Katz would want to say that while the meaning of a word such as 'bachelor' may slightly vary on occasions of use, and while the word may be more frequently used in some situations than others, these are matters to do with linguistic performance, the use of words and expressions, which it is not their business to account for. Their analysis attempts to model the semantic competence available to all native speakers in a society which allows them to use the word 'bachelor' in an acceptable way in sentences. Now much hinges on the word 'acceptable' here, because some modern linguists would want to make more of this and argue that acceptability is not just a question of producing sentences which are comprehensible sentences in a language, but also of using expressions aptly in the light of, for example, social conventions. This in turn has led to an erosion (which is by no means complete or uncontroversial) of the distinction between competence and performance, and a concern to specify such matters as what Fillmore calls the 'happiness conditions' for the apt use of an expression (see Fillmore, 1971). The reason for this erosion, however, is not some high-minded concern to start taking account of factors affecting linguistic performance, it stems from various inadequacies which result from ignoring such matters when pursuing more traditional linguistic aims.

Although linguists' purposes are very different from those of the sociologist, their approach suggests some ways in which it might be possible to decide on the meanings of words and expressions and to isolate the central dictionary meaning of any item. If such an endeavour were relevant for sociological purposes, if, by eliminating the ambiguity from the central meanings of the words used, it could resolve our problem of deciding which formulation of the extract from Sudnow was the most likely, then we could surely arrive at some unequivocal formulation of what was going on in the sequence between the PD and his client. If, on the other hand, the assumptions and implications of this kind of attempt to decide on the central meaning of items are inappropriate for sociological purposes, some alternative way will have to be found for deciding on the adequate formulation of any stretch of talk. It is for these reasons that Chapter 2 of this book is particularly concerned with anthropological attempts, heavily influenced by linguistics, to use sense discriminations of lexical items in tackling anthropological problems.

Philosophical discussions of meaning have traditionally polarised around two camps, the realists and the nominalists, realists contending that things to which we apply the same name have common essential properties by which we can identify them, nominalists that they have nothing in common other than the convention which we have learned to apply to them.[7] In the latter part of the nineteenth and the early part of the twentieth centuries the realists reigned supreme, although different writers answered the question of 'What is the meaning of X?' in diverse ways. The tendency in the writing of J. S. Mill and Russell was to see sentences as collections of names – names which referred to features of the external world. The reading taken from Mill, for example, was that words stood to sentence meanings as atoms to molecules, and that all words, or nearly all words, were names for things. To mean anything, therefore, was to denote something, to find out the meaning of a word or descriptive phrase was to find the referent; therefore to speak of the meaning of phrases like 'the hundredth man to stand on the top of Mount Everest', one had to invoke some sort of tied concept which was being denoted and to which the phrase referred (Mill, 1843).[8] Other writers such as Frege and Meinong answered the question of 'What is the meaning of X?' more along the lines of Locke. The meaning of a linguistic expression was the idea for which the expression acted as an indicator; thus Frege held that abstract entities called 'senses' were expressed by the meaningful expressions of any language. Philosophy itself was conceived by men like Brentano, Husserl and Meinong as concerned with a realm of meanings, thought objects, a realm which was distinctly philosophical in character and thus distinguished from other fields such as psychology.

The reference or naming theory has come under severe scrutiny in the course of this century, culminating in the later philosophy of Wittgenstein (1953, 1958). A variety of arguments has been relevant here, some of which are given below. It is possible to use two descriptive phrases to refer to a given object, but we might want to say that these phrases have different meanings so that the common object cannot be what both these phrases mean; Ryle (1963) gives the example of 'the morning star' and 'the evening star' as different ways of referring to Venus. Clearly a referential theory will only be adequate as a general theory if all meaningful linguistic expressions do refer to something, but this is not the case. Little words like 'and', 'if' and 'is' obviously create problems here, and for this reason are usually banished by reference theorists to some special class of their own. Yet if we say, ' "If" means *provided that*', it is not clear that we are not giving some account of the meaning of 'if'; moreover it is one which does not appear to trade on a referent.⁹ One of Wittgenstein's main lines of attack was to show that learning the meaning of a word is not synonymous with learning the referent of a word, and that a theory of ostensive definition is inadequate as a general theory. To point to an object and utter the name of it seems potentially to work best as an account of how children come to attach meaning to certain rather concrete sorts of words such as 'kitten', 'fridge', and 'cow'. But, even with these words, when an adult points to a cat and says 'kitty' a capacity to work out what the adult is pointing at is presumed, whereas this is always ambiguous in the act of pointing.

> One can ostensively define a proper name, the name of a colour, the name of a material, a numeral, the name of a point of the compass and so on. The definition of the number two. 'That is called "two" ' – pointing to two nuts – is perfectly exact. – But how can two be defined like that? The person one gives the definition to doesn't know what one wants to call 'two'; he will suppose that 'two' is the name given to *this* group of nuts! – He *may* suppose this; but perhaps he does not . . . An ostensive definition can be variously interpreted in *every* case.
> [Wittgenstein, 1953, para. 28]¹⁰

Wittgenstein's mature solution to the problem of meaning, then, is to reject the notion of meanings as entities and to stress how any analysis of meaning must be bound up with the variety of uses of an expression. This led him to an interesting attempt to supersede the nominalist–realist dichotomy. Take the example of the word 'game'. Nominalists claim that games have nothing in common except that they are called 'games', realists that they must have something in common other than that they are called 'games'. Wittgenstein is in partial agreement and partial disagreement with each position. On the one hand, he argues, games do not have a list of features which are common if we consider the variety of uses of that term; but at the same time their referents are not arbitrary in the sense that the use of such words is conventionally bound to particular forms of life, so that it is a justifiable and accountable matter to use the expression on any given occasion (see Bambrough, 1966).

In many ways Wittgenstein's negative views *vis-à-vis* previous philosophical discussion were clearer and more extensive than his positive views. On the more positive side, Austin's writings (1961, 1962) have been at least as influential on subsequent developments in the philosophy of language, and his writings are the more direct precursors of some of the views which will be dealt with in this book. If a large number of expressions do not gain their meaning by referring to things, they must gain their meaning by *doing* other sorts of things, and much of Austin's writing is given over to an attempt to separate analytically utterances or dimensions of utterances which say or state something ('constatives' in Austin's early work) from those utterances which in their uttering actually perform an act and which are not subject to truth – falsity criteria of evaluation – statements like 'I promise to marry you' (performatives). These distinctions will be explored in more detail in Chapter 3; at present it is only necessary to note that, in pursuing this goal of distinguishing utterances which do different sorts of things, some philosophers have been concerned to give an explicit account of what it is to perform a particular speech act such as a promise. As the meaning of such utterances is not given by the referents of the words, but is bound up with the context in which the utterance takes place, accounts of what is involved in performing a speech act will have to incorporate aspects of this context in their analysis. So Searle (1969, Chapter 3) provides us with a set of conditions which, he argues, we take to be fulfilled if we hear a statement as being a promise; conditions which refer to such contextual matters as the speaker's intentions. Thus one of Searle's conditions for promising is that if S promises to buy me something tomorrow, and I hear him as promising, then one of the conditions that is fulfilled is that I also believe that S *intends* to buy me something tomorrow. What we have here is another kind of attempt to account for the meaning of an utterance, for deciding what sort of utterance an utterance is, according to a set of rules. In its inclusion of contextual features it is of course quite different from the Fodor/Katz model in linguistics, and in fact there has been a good deal of argument in recent years over the relative merits of the philosophical and linguistic approaches to the analysis of meaning.[11] For our purposes, however, they are similar in that they both offer the possibility of extracting unambiguous formulations of the meaning of stretches of conversation in an explicit, methodical way, and for this reason I shall be taking a closer look at some of Searl's claims as regards promising in Chapter 3.

One apparent contradiction in the later philosophical discussions of meaning is worth pointing out now. The tendency of later writers such as Searle has been to interpret Wittgenstein's positive views on meaning, the doctrine of meaning as use, as holding that the meaning of words and utterances is their ordinary, *standard* meaning in a linguistic community. For this reason Searle takes care to say that he is dealing with standard promises, not fringe or marginal ones. So these writers have proceeded as if standard meanings of various kinds can be identified and distinguished according to a fairly specific set of rules such that necessary and sufficient conditions for the appropriate use of a word or utterance can be extracted. Caton (1971) has noted, I think correctly, that it often seems to be assumed without discussion that the more radical position held by Wittgenstein is incorrect. Much of Wittgenstein's writing is concerned to show that attempts to specify fixed entities or fixed criteria for the meaning of expressions are unlikely to be fruitful. For these reasons I see the work of the ethnomethodologists as bearing a close resemblance to the later Wittgenstein, but as diverging markedly from many later developments in the philosophy of language.

The aim of this first chapter has been to present a preliminary view of the controversy which will be dealt with in the book, and to present it in the context of sociological research in such a way that it becomes clear that the controversy has some bearing on the way in which we as sociologists are entitled to proceed in sociological enquiry. I have concentrated on giving a sketch of intellectual developments in linguistics and philosophy because, although most sociology students will probably have had little contact with these disciplines, they have significantly influenced and underpinned sociological and anthropological investigations of language. My argument has been that the question of whether we can arrive at unequivocal formulations of stretches of talk is linked to the question of whether we can devise a systematic procedure for recovering the meaning of expressions, and the extent to which this is possible depends on the way in which the meaning of expressions is related to the words used to make statements and to the context in which statements are made. I have noted that some philosophers and linguists argue that the meaning of the words we use has specifiable distinctive features or that the meaning of our utterances is related to the contexts in which they occur in some rule-based way. Over the course of Chapters 2 and 3 I shall examine more carefully the merits and disadvantages of supposing that the meaning of expressions can be extracted in such a manner.

2

Components of Meaning

In many ways componential analysis, as employed by anthropologists, is a continuation and extension of the Sapir-Whorf interest
in using language as a way of exploring the particular perspectives
on the world contained within a culture. It is more limited in that
most analyses have been of sets of lexical items, the vocabulary of
a language, whereas Whorf also attempted to relate features of
syntax and grammar to forms of conceptualisation (see Carroll,
1956). In other ways, however, it is more elaborate in that a more
systematic effort is made to plot the primary dimensions of meaning
along which any two vocabulary items differ, and it also displays a
greater awareness of the problematic relationship between any such
description and the cognition of members of a culture.[1] In general,
componential analysis attempts to extract the rules which underlie
the way in which people order phenomena in a culture, to derive
these rules directly from language itself, and to set out the distinctive
semantic features of items which differentiate them from other items
at any particular level of analysis. The methodology by which the
semantic features of words are arrived at is a structuralist one and,
as well as influencing the nature of this methodology, linguists have
also adopted componential analysis as a way of coping with the
problem of semantic description. For example the approach of
Fodor and Katz, which I briefly outlined in Chapter 1, draws heavily
on such procedures. The structuralist strategy is characterised by a
concern to plot the ways in which one item *differs* in meaning from
other items, and we shall see that the aim of such analysis for
linguists is an idealised model of the knowledge which is required
in order to use a term appropriately in the context of sentences
which are acceptable linguistic units within a culture. The aims of
anthropologists who use this form of analysis have been stated more

strongly. For example some see the results of the technique as enabling them to know when and where to use a particular term. But before considering these aims and evaluating them in greater detail I want to work through a relatively straightforward example in order to familiarise the reader with this kind of analysis.

The example of Palaung pronouns is taken from an interesting and highly readable book by Burling (1970, Chapter 1). Palaung is a language spoken by a small tribe in the northern Shan States of Burma, and like other languages it has a small set of terms that act as personal pronouns. This set of terms is more complex, however, than the first, second, and third person singular and plural to which we are accustomed, as can be seen from the list below:

1 'I'
2 'thou' (i.e. 'you' singular, without the archaic/ecclesiastical connotations of English 'thou')
3 'he, she' (i.e. 3rd person singular with no distinction for sex)
4 'he or she, and I' (i.e. one other person and I)
5 'thou and I'
6 'they and I'
7 'thou, I, and he, she, or they' (i.e. the person spoken to, the speaker and one more additional person)
8 'he or she, and thou'
9 'they and thou'
10 'they two' (i.e. 3rd person dual)
11 'they, thou or more'

Thus, whereas in English we have three plural pronouns, Palaung has eight, and in English numbers 4, 5, 6 and 7 would all have to be translated as 'we'. Now in accord with the structuralist approach we must find some way of showing how the meaning and range of application of each of these terms differ from each other, particularly as we cannot illuminate their meaning too well through our own pronoun usage. One way of doing this is to extract dimensions of meaning along which the pronouns can be ordered. In common with our own pronouns one such dimension would be number, but whereas our pronouns can be distinguished on a simple singular/plural dichotomy, the Palaung pronouns clearly require a triadic distinction of singulars (numbers 1, 2 and 3), duals (4, 5, 8 and 10) and plurals (6, 7, 9 and 11). But this ordering into sets still leaves certain pronouns semantically undifferentiated (e.g. 1, 2 and 3), so we can go on to distinguish two further dimensions of meaning which can be used for the purpose of ordering. First, certain terms include the speaker (1, 4, 5, 6 and 7), while others do not (all the rest). Second, certain terms include the person being spoken to, the hearer (2, 5, 7, 8, and 9), while others do not (all the rest). In Table 2.1 it is shown that, if we sort these eleven pronouns simultaneously along these three dimensions, we are then able to distinguish any pair of pronouns on at least one dimension of meaning, or, put another way, each pronoun can be given a unique semantic description by the intersection of the semantic components from each dimension.

Table 2.1. *Palaung Pronouns*

	Speaker Included	Speaker Not Included
Hearer Included	5 (dual) 7 (plural)	2 (singular) 8 (dual) 9 (plural)
Hearer Not Included	1 (singular 4 (dual) 6 (plural)	3 (singular) 10 (dual) 11 (plural)

(From Burling, 1970. Reproduced by permission of Holt, Rinehart & Winston.)

Thus pronoun 5 could be semantically defined as dual + hearer + speaker, pronoun 3 as singular – speaker – hearer, and so on.

Technically this sort of arrangement is known as a paradigm; that is, a way of ordering lexical items where we are dealing with multiple dimensions which intersect. The example is a simple one, but using this technique much more complex analyses have been carried out, notably in the field of kinship studies. Goodenough,[2] for example, has provided such an analysis of his own kinship terminology in which five dimensions of semantic contrast distinguish the majority of kinship terms from each other; and it has been shown that quite complex arrays of lexical items can be elegantly discriminated, each from the rest, on the basis of quite limited numbers of semantic dimensions.

Paradigms are just one type of componential analysis, however, and the main example on which I shall draw in this chapter takes an alternative form, that of a taxonomy. It also relates to a set of lexical items whose sociological relevance may be more apparent, namely disease terms. The example is provided by Frake's discussion of disease among the Subanun who live on the island of

Mindinao in the Phillipines (1961). These people have 132 diagnostic categories of illness which possess unique single-word labels, and Frake presents an analysis of the ways in which members of that society define these categories as being hierarchially arranged, and of the sorts of criterial features held by members to distinguish the categories at any given level of the hierarchy. His diagrammatic representation of this hierarchy together with the criterial features relevant to a particular class of skin diseases called 'sores' is given below as Table 2.2. Frake argues that for his informants there was a high degree of verbal consensus[3] on the fact that 'simple sores', for example, and 'distal ulcers' were sub-types of 'beldut' and that the distinction between them operated at a specific level of contrast,

Table 2.2. *Criterial Contrasts Differentiating 'Sores'*

	beldut 'sore'					
	telemaw 'distal ulcer'		baga 'proximal ulcer'			
	telemaw glai 'shallow distal ulcer'	telemaw glibun 'deep distal ulcer'	baga 'shallow proximal ulcer'	begwak 'deep proximal ulcer'	beldut 'simple sore'	selim-bunut 'multiple sore'
depth	sh	dp	sh	dp		
distality	distal		proximal			
severity	severe				mild	
spread	single					mult

(From Frake, 1961. Reproduced by permission of the American Anthropological Association.)

along the dimension of the degree of severity of the sore. Notice how 'simple sores' and 'sores' are both given the same name, 'beldut'. Clearly, terms can have more than one sense, so that they may be taken to contrast with different items at different levels of analysis. Thus our own term 'man' may contrast with woman, boy, unmanly males and animals at different levels of analysis. Frake argues that if the context of use does not make the level of contrast clear, his informants would be capable of being more verbally specific about the precise way in which the word is being used.

The major difference between a taxonomy of this kind and our earlier example of a paradigm is that the semantic distinctions employed in one segment of a taxonomy do not necessarily apply to other segments. Put in another way, whereas we were able to characterise the whole set of pronouns in terms of all the semantic dimensions being employed in the analysis, this is not a feature of Frake's classification where, for example, simple sores are not characterised along the dimensions of distality and depth. Nevertheless we can still formally describe the criterial features of any particular diagnostic category, thus ascribing to them specific components. Thus 'begwak' could be described as + depth − distality + severity − spread, and so on.

So the structuralist approach to meaning, as embodied in componential analysis, involves locating one item relative to another by demonstrating how items differ from each other along various dimensions of meaning, and by giving each item a semantic description according to the number of components of various dimensions required to differentiate it from other items. Furthermore, this mode of procedure may bear some resemblance to the way in which we arrive at the meaning of words. Conklin (1955), for example, when he began his study of the classification of colours among the Hanunóo of the Phillipines, was baffled by their colour terms until he asked informants to contrast specimens instead of asking them to define isolated ones, and only in this way was he able to discover that their system seemed to be founded on different axes from our own. Clearly, any evaluation of such work is tied closely to the aims of investigators, and I want to begin such an evaluation by considering the aims of linguists who have recently made use of this approach.

For Lyons 'componential analysis is a technique for the economical statement of certain semantic relations between lexical items and between sentences containing them' (1968, p. 476). For example, a componential analysis of the words 'men' and 'women' should predict certain relationships between sentences. It should predict the relationship of entailment between the two sentences in (1) below, the relationship of incompatibility and inconsistency in (2) and the tautological nature of (3).[4]

(1) 'The secretary is a woman.' 'The secretary is an adult.'
(2) 'The secretary is a woman.' 'The secretary is a man.'
(3) 'That man is an adult.'

Going just a little further, it is possible to see the alternative of describing a word as ± MALE as being dependent on a prior description of an item such as + ANIMATE, so that by this means we can account for a combination like 'female book' being as unacceptable as 'female man'. In the context of Palaung pronouns the analysis would have linguistic payoff if it allowed one to predict sentences where, for example, the meaning of the sentence would not be changed by the substitution of one pronoun for another and where the selection rules accounting for such a phenomenon might be more elegantly stated by componential analysis than by an alternative technique.

There is one problematic area of componential analysis for both linguists and anthropologists, however, which is crucial in any evaluation of the technique, and this concerns the relation of decontextualised meanings of words to situations of use. The problem, stated more explicitly, is this. While it is undoubtedly possible to elicit distinctive features of words,[5] as our own examples above suggest, it may nevertheless be argued that the meaning of a word in any given instance is bound up in significant ways with the context in which an utterance is made. Let me illustrate the point from Frake's own discussion of Subanun disease categories. Frake argues that the Subanun distinguish verbally between different kinds of sores on the basis of such features as distality, severity and spread, but he also admits that the presence or absence of such features in any specific case is by no means clearcut. The Subanun do not use high-precision measuring instruments to resolve these issues, and in order to 'use' such features sensibly in diagnosis (in order to understand the meaning of the various terms involved), one would need to spend some time with these people gaining an idea of how to employ the features. In doing this, one would be learning something of the kinds of knowledge and reasoning procedures used to warrant the decision that a criterial feature was present or absent in a particular case. Without having the detail to draw on for the Subanun, it might be more appropriate to illustrate this in connection with our own distinction between 'riot' and 'demonstration'. Let us suppose that *one* criterial feature of a riot is that laws are being broken. In specific cases, presumably, when deciding how to use this feature, we would have to ask ourselves such questions as: 'Are they breaking the law of necessity or voluntarily? Does the breaking of *any* law by *any* number of participants warrant the presence of this criterial feature?' In some cases, at least, the answers to such questions are considered sufficiently ambiguous to merit resort to legal inquiry in an effort to characterise adequately the nature of disturbances.[6] The argument then is that the 'seeing'

B

of a criterial feature in any instance is problematic in that it relies on a speaker's judgement as to whether a set of phenomena constitute a criterial feature. In these circumstances, it can be argued, the speaker will always be taking into account contextual matters in making such judgements, and the judgements themselves will be defeasible.[7]

This kind of argument is, of course, foreseen by linguists and they guard against it in a variety of ways. I would like here to note the way in which Lyons guards himself, as the set of assumptions he makes bears some resemblance to those of the sociologist in dealing with abstract de-contextualised meanings. Two of Lyons' arguments concern us here. In the first, and more important, he recognises that in a conversation a prior set of utterances can act as a significant context for, and give meaning to, an utterance which follows. He goes on:

> The limiting case of contexts which have not 'developed' in this sense would be those in which the participants in a conversation do not draw upon their previous knowledge of one another or the information communicated in earlier utterances, but where they share the more general beliefs, conventions and presuppositions governing the particular 'universe of discourse' in the society to which they belong. Such contexts, which we will refer to as *restricted contexts*, are comparatively rare, since most utterances depend for their understanding upon the information contained in previous utterances . . . Since we cannot in general identify either the actual elements 'selected' by the speaker in the production of utterances or all the relevant features of particular contexts, we can make it a matter of methodological decision to do what linguists have generally done in practice; and that is to handle the semantic relationships between the sentences from which they are assumed to be 'derived' when they are produced by native speakers in restricted contexts.
> [1968, pp. 419–20]

This quotation provides us with some insight into the assumptions of the structuralist approach to the analysis of sense relations. It admits that for the linguist, as for the anthropologist, the typical approach is one which attempts to extract, or relies on, a subject's general cultural competence in assigning meaning to a word independently of particular occasions of its use. At the same time there is a further assumption that sense relations, so defined, inform in some way the meanings of expressions on occasions of their use, and this is where Lyons' second argument comes in. He argues that to arrive at the 'fully-determined meaning' of words is not a realistic goal, particularly as:

> . . . the way in which language is used in normal situations can be explained on the much weaker assumption that the speakers of the language are in sufficient agreement about the 'use' of words (what they refer to, what they imply, etc.) to prevent misunderstandings.
> [1968, p. 412]

In the case of componential analysis, Lyons' argument seems to imply that if, in the case of the Subanun, we had Frake's analysis at our disposal, the analysis might be taken as successful if it allowed us to use disease terms without generating misunderstanding on the part of hearers. In this argument, clearly, much hinges on just what is meant by 'misunderstanding'. Suppose I wanted to sell a chair, and after I have placed an advertisement in a newspaper someone comes to the door and says, 'I've come about a chair.' Assume that I have done a componential analysis of the word 'chair' and on that basis can assign a semantic description to that word in this utterance. The problem is, however, that I do not hear this utterance as referring to any old chair but to a very specific chair, the one that I advertised, and if I did not hear it in that way then one could surely expect considerable misunderstanding. Here, of course, I am not dealing with a 'restricted context' (to use Lyons' terms) for it is clear that the prior advertisement informs the utterance in a significant way. But as restricted contexts, according to Lyons himself, are rare, this hardly affects our evaluation as to whether the analysis will allow us to avoid misunderstanding 'in normal situations'.

If we take it as our task to gain access to de-contextualised meanings of words, one problem which we face is how to go about extracting such meanings. The problem is twofold. First, we have to be fairly sure that the context from which we extract such information is not unduly influencing in some way the nature of that information. Second, we have to be sure that the information gained (in Frake's case information about the criteria by which disease categories are differentiated) is the only correct information, and that other ways of distinguishing the lexical items would not work just as well. Both these points have raised problems for com-

ponential analysis. As regards the first question, it is difficult for us
to examine its relevance to Frake's analysis as he extracted his information by intelligent questioning of the Subanun, asking them to
describe differences between diseases and so on, but he does not
give us systematic information about the nature of his questions.
Later and more explicit investigation, however, does reveal how
the data-gathering context may influence the nature of the data.
Ariel (1967), for example, makes a number of pertinent points here
in connection with Bendix's attempt to construct componential
analyses of various verbs (1966). One of the techniques used by
Bendix was to present his informants with a sentence in which two
words were contrasted, and the informants were then asked to make
a free interpretation of the sentence. On the basis of this information
Bendix makes a preliminary attempt to define the meanings of the
verbs concerned. One of the items which Ariel discusses is the
sentence 'He did not lie, he sat.' Ariel suggests that 'contact' and 'no
contact' is a relevant property of the semantic relation between the
two clauses (i.e. 'His back was in contact with it' is an interpretation
which might be made of the test sentence), and that 'contact' or 'no
contact' could be defined therefore as relevant features of the
semantic structure of the verbs 'lie' and 'sat' respectively. But he
writes:

> One cannot rule out the possibility that the informant gives the
> above interpretation not because he is compelled by his language
> to make the distinction, but because he is tempted to do so by the
> form of the test and other factors. The contrast exposed by the
> test can influence him to think only of the extreme situation in
> which 'lie' and 'lie flat' are identical. The irrelevant fact that one
> cannot just lie flat unless there is something to support him is then
> apt to become mistaken for a semantic feature.
> [1967, p. 541]

The second problem is even more challenging, and concerns
whether or not the results of a componential analysis can be taken
as valid. The problem is that at any given level of contrast two
lexical items may be discriminated in a variety of ways, all of which
in some sense may be correct or culturally appropriate. If this is
the case, how then do we identify the components of meaning which
distinguish the main or central sense of these items? The problem is
empirically documented by Perchonock and Werner with Navaho
informants (1969). They gave these informants a set of cards with

the names of a large number of foods eaten by the Navaho, and they asked them to sort the cards into categories in any way they felt appropriate. After they had constructed a number of categories, the informants were asked to sub-divide these categories, and so on until the finest possible sub-divisions had been achieved. There was a good deal of variation in the types of classification arrived at by informants, but what was most interesting was that informants agreed as to the correctness of other people's classifications, even though they differed considerably from their own. Among linguists, there seems to be a tendency either to resolve this problem by taking as the valid/correct system of classification the system which constitutes a psychological reality for informants, or by selecting the analysis which is most elegant and economical in format.[8] For our purposes, however, the problem remains. If any item can be distinguished from some other item within a given semantic domain in terms of more than one set of criteria, we are theoretically required to take account of the procedure by which the *relevant* contrasts are arrived at. If someone claims that a group of people is a mob rather than a collection of individuals, we need to know *which* sense of these terms is being contrasted, and the answer will be unclear from a componential analysis which provides us with information concerning only a limited number of the ways in which the sense of items can be said to contrast with each other.

I mentioned earlier that for Lyons one aim of componential analysis was to provide us with a semantic description of words which was sufficient to allow for their use without involving misunderstanding on the part of others; but stronger aims have been expressed by anthropologists using this analysis. Conklin (1964) recognises three criteria for evaluating the adequacy of such analysis: (1) productivity (in terms of appropriate anticipation, if not actual prediction), (2) replicability or testability, and (3) economy. The first will most concern us here, and is supported by many as a goal which, even if not yet fully realised, is one which may be aspired to. One main goal of componential analysis, therefore, is to allow us to predict when and where it will be appropriate for us to describe some object or person in a particular way. Going back to the Subanun's ulcers, Frake's analysis, if it were fully adequate, should allow us to know when and where it is appropriate to describe a particular ulcer, for example, as a 'begwak'. There seem to me at least three sorts of difficulties here.[9]

The first problem can be stated generally as follows. If for any particular instance more than one description could be considered as a correct description according to the componential analysis, then how does one appropriately select one term rather than another? This again is a problem acknowledged in the literature on componential analysis, but let me illustrate it with the Subanun. On the basis of Table 2.2 it would be correct to describe a particular sore as either 'beldut' or 'telemaw' or 'telemaw glai', but one could argue that there might be quite systematic variations as regards which of these terms was selected. In fact Frake reports an example concerning an infectious swelling of his leg in a way which suggests that such variations are systematic (1961, pp. 117–18). He reports that some people who wished to avoid detailed discussion of his ills in favour of some other subject would simply describe his swelling as a 'skin disease' ('nuka'), while others, the 'taxonomic hair-splitters' as he calls them, would be much more precise in their diagnosis, perhaps describing it as an inflamed 'quasi-bite' ('pagid'); and yet other people fell somewhere in between these two extremes. The same systematic variation in the use of correct terms is noted forcefully in Schegloff's discussion of spatial locations (1972). In describing our position at any point in time to another person, a number of 'correct' descriptions are potentially open for an answer to the question 'Where are you?' If I was holidaying in the north of Greece, I could answer such a question by saying, 'in the north', 'on holiday in Greece', or even 'at the end of the corridor'. All of these answers might count as correct descriptions. Yet our selection between them is a systematic one; it takes account, among other things, of the knowledge which we expect the other person to have already of our whereabouts, and of the sort of knowledge necessary for their purposes in the light of what sort of person they are. In other words, the selection of one correct description rather than another seems to be systematically related to the context in which the description takes place. If the anthropologist's aim is to provide us with an analysis which will allow us to know when and where to use a term, he must also provide us with some procedures for the appropriate selection of one correct term rather than another. The most obvious solution to the problem is to provide us with some characterisation of the contexts in which the use of a term is more appropriate, at which point the analysis will be taking the form of a more conventional sociolinguistic analysis, in which variations in some linguistic item are mapped on to variations in contextual features which supposedly constrain the use of the item. In Chapter 3 I shall be discussing in detail an attempt to do this in connection with the nineteenth-century Russian *ty/vy* alternation (similar to the French *tu/vous* alternation).

The second difficulty I want to stress is that if the componential analysis is to allow us as hearers to hear utterances in the way that native hearers hear utterances, and to attach meaning to utterances in the way that they do, then further information must be provided as to how we as hearers are to sort out what a speaker is *doing* when making an utterance. Again the problem can be illustrated from Frake's paper. He writes:

> Although not explicitly stated, judgement of severity is, *in fact*, partially a function of social role contingencies. Do the patient and his consultants wish to emphasise the former's crippling disability, which prevents him from discharging an expected obligation? Or do they wish to communicate that the patient's lesion is not serious enough to interfere with his duties? Diagnosis is not an automatic response to pathological stimuli; it is a social activity whose results hinge in part on role-playing strategies.
> [1961, pp. 128–9]

If someone makes a statement about a sore, therefore, as well as hearing the claim as a correct or an incorrect one we also consider what sort of statement they are making. Some statements which on the surface may appear candidates for descriptive diagnoses may in fact be heard as judgements or suggestions. Consider, in another context, the artificial example below:

Mother: That cough sounds much worse today. It's going to your chest.
Child: Well I'm not staying in again, so there!

Even if the relevant componential analyses are carried out for all the words in an utterance therefore, there is a further problem if we are to hear and attribute meaning to utterances in the way that native hearers do in particular contexts. This problem requires an analyst to provide procedures by which we as hearers can understand what is being done by a speaker with an utterance. Whether such procedures can be provided, whether speech acts such as referring and promising can be identified according to a set of explicit rules, will also be considered in Chapter 3.

The third point concerns the way in which componential analysis leads us to think of the application of words to things. If the mean-

ing of a word is bound up with its criterial features, this suggests
that if a word is used where the criterial features are not present its
use will be problematic in some sense. But this does not seem to be
the case necessarily, as Frake himself tells us in connection with his
leg wound :

> . . . an informant insisted that an inflammation on my leg was an
> inflamed insect bite rather than an inflamed wound . . . even
> though I told him I thought it originated as a 'minor cut'. I
> simply, according to him, had not noticed the prodromal bite.
> In such cases the existence of the prodrome is deduced from its
> criteriality to a diagnosis eventually arrived at on other grounds.
> [1961, p. 126]

From this instance it is clear that a diagnosis can be arrived at on
grounds other than those suggested by criterial features. At the
same time the criterial features play a powerful part in the informant's discussion with Frake, as they are used as prescriptions
for reconstructing what must have occurred.[10] Criterial features
therefore appear to be both weaker and stronger than componential
analysis would suggest. On the one hand, direct evidence of criterial
features is not necessary in order for a particular diagnosis to be
arrived at; yet, on the other hand, this does not prevent their being
used as a basis for inferring what must have occurred at some
earlier stage in the illness. The part which criterial features play in
diagnosis, therefore, is going to be complex, and if componential
analysis leads us to think of diagnosis as a pairing of a set of
criterial features with a verbal label then the model is going to be
a highly over-simplified one.

Any assessment of componential analysis must be tied up with
the aims of the investigator using the analysis, and in this chapter I
have distinguished three such aims. The aim of most linguists using
the technique is to account for certain semantic relations within a
sentence or between sentences; for example, to help us to account
systematically for why it is that 'His typewriter has bad intentions'[11]
is a semantically anomalous sentence in some sense. None of the
arguments that I have advanced is intended seriously to cast doubt
on such endeavours, though some of them, such as my argument
that data extraction techniques often constrain the results of the
componential analysis, will have bearing on specific investigations.
A second aim which I considered was whether a componential
analysis allowed us to use and understand a word without generating

misunderstanding. There were two difficulties here. First, the notion of misunderstanding was unclear. The example discussed was the case of someone calling about 'a chair' in response to my advertisement. I may be able to understand what they say when they use the word 'chair', and even assign a semantic description on the basis of the componential analysis, so that in this sense the situation does not lead to misunderstanding. But it will lead to misunderstanding if by that we mean that there would be some confusion if I were not to hear the use of the word 'chair', in this case, as referring to a very specific chair. Here, however, the second difficulty comes in, for if I am to hear the word as referring to a specific chair then one needs to take account of the way in which the context gives meaning to the word, but this task is excluded on theoretical grounds by writers such as Lyons, who insists on dealing with de-contextualised meanings of words in what he calls 'restricted contexts'.

The anthropologist's aim was that the componential analysis should allow a speaker to know when and where to use a particular term appropriately within a given culture. There are numerous stumbling blocks to this. The criterial or distinctive features of expressions such as 'sores' are not unambiguously present on any specific occasion, so that a further competence to recognise such features is presumed. Furthermore, in Frake's case, and in our everyday lives, there are instances where we infer criterial characteristics from the very terms which these characteristics are supposed to warrant on the basis of the componential analysis, so that our use of terms in appropriate ways extends well beyond the ways which componential analysis suggests. Several of our criticisms here led to interesting questions concerning the way in which a context may be systematically related to the use and meaning of an expression. It was argued in Frake's case that, according to the componential analysis, there could at any one time be several correct ways of describing a sore, and the question raised was whether the selection of a term may be related in some rule-governed way to the context in which the term is used. A second argument concerned the way in which an expression gained its meaning from the sort of utterance which contained it. This raised the question of whether it is possible to model our competence as hearers to recognise speech acts such as referring and promising. If this can be done, then we may be able to supplement the componential analysis in such a way that the goal of an unambiguous hearing of any particular utterance is more closely approximated. These two arguments constitute the main theme of Chapter 3.

B*

Finally, I want to return to the problem in Chapter 1 which led into this discussion. The problem was to provide an adequate formulation for any stretch of talk. The ambiguities which I unravelled were not the sorts of ambiguities which linguists have been concerned with – ambiguities like 'His typewriter has bad intentions', where there is a clearcut misuse of the conventional semantic relations embodied in our language. The ambiguities stemmed from the possibility of constructing several distinct, but conventionally plausible, interpretations of the nature of the talk. A componential analysis alone is not able to resolve these ambiguities for us, since it leaves unexamined such matters as the way in which we as hearers distinguish utterances which are cooling people out from those which are simply offering advice, or the nature of the competence being drawn on in order for a person to define a case as a normal crime. Without some explicit account of such matters we are no nearer assigning an adequate interpretation to the talk.[12]

3

Rules, Norms and Speech Acts

While I have highlighted some difficulties in characterising the
meaning of words according to rules, it is still possible to defend a
rule-based approach to the analysis of speech events. In Chapter 2
I raised the problem of how a choice between one term or another
is made, when both could in a sense be used, and one answer to
this problem is to specify in detail the kinds of contexts which
appear to be associated with a person's selection of one term rather
than another, in order to arrive at sociolinguistic selection rules.
This chapter begins with an examination of one such attempt to
systematise contextual influences on selection. Then I shall examine
some attempts by philosophers and linguists to develop a rule-based
approach to the analysis of utterances, particularly those which,
through Austin's influence, have come to be known as illocutionary
acts. Lastly, I shall attempt to relate these issues to a wider discussion of the notion of norms and rules as employed in sociology.

The correlation of contextual features with linguistic variants has
been a popular endeavour for sociolinguists over the last decade.
Hymes (1962) set out the clearest programmatic statements in the
field, and suggested that social variation in speech use might be
located along such dimensions as the kind of speech event being
engaged in (e.g. sales talk as compared with man-to-man talk), the
roles of the various parties (e.g. talk to children compared with talk
to adults), the topic of the discussion (e.g. children's talk about
toys compared with their talk about discipline), the style of the
discussion (e.g. whether informal or formal). Hymes raises several
questions in connection with such variations. Some are more sociological, as when he asks what part a speech event such as 'cussing
out' plays in the maintenance of a social system. His main reason
for considering such features, however, is to identify contexts which

limit the range of meaning which may be attached to an expression. He writes:

> The use of a linguistic form identifies a range of meanings. A context can support a range of meanings. When a form is used in a context it eliminates the meanings possible to that context other than those that form can signal; the context eliminates from consideration the meanings possible to the form other than those that context can support.
> [1962, p. 19]

Frake's attempt to extract the contrastive features of terms within a diagnostic context, which I discussed in Chapter 2, would fall very much in line with Hyme's aims. In later sociolinguistic work, however, the explicit concern of linking the extraction of contextual features with semantic analysis has dwindled. Labov's early studies in New York (1966) laid the foundation for much of this work. Working with linguistic items defined at a phonological level, for example, he found interesting social class and contextual variations in the stress patterns used in the pronunciation of certain words by his informants. For instance, lower class informants in his New York sample used the pre-consonantal (r) in words like *guard* more frequently when reading out a list of words than when engaging in casual speech. In the latter case they were more likely to pronounce the word as *gad*. At a different linguistic level of analysis Brown and Ford (1964) have demonstrated variations in the kinds of contextual features which lead one to address a person by his first name (e.g. *Andy*) or title plus last name (e.g. *Mr X*). There were similar indications in Chapter 2 that while a number of disease terms could be selected as correct descriptions of any sore, the selection between them would turn out to be systematic, and influenced by various aspects of the context in which the utterance was made. I now want to explore this kind of selection in more detail and to consider how valuable these selection rules will be in any analysis of what people say.

As an example of such rules I want to take Friedrich's discussion of the features which governed the selection between the personal pronouns *ty* and *vy* among nineteenth-century Russian gentry (1966). The distinction is similar to the French distinction between *tu* and *vous*, the former being associated with more intimate, familiar relationships, the latter with more formal relationships. In fact the (T) (V) distinction in Russian only began during the eighteenth century, when French customs and the French language became increasingly influential in educated circles. The advantage of taking the Russian variation is that Friedrich provides us with a wealth of conversational material in which we can examine for ourselves the selection between (T) and (V), though one has to bear in mind that the source of his data is nineteenth-century Russian novels, not recorded conversations. Ervin-Tripp (1971) has tried to formalise for us the contextual features which, according to Friedrich, constrain the use of (T) and (V) in these novels, and Fig. 3.1 is her diagrammatic representation of these constraints and of the way in which they interact with each other.

Fig. 3.1 is not claimed to be a model of decision procedures employed by Russians when selecting (T) or (V). It is, according to Ervin-Tripp, a logical model of 'the structure implicit in people's knowledge of what forms of address are possible and appropriate'. (1971, p. 18).

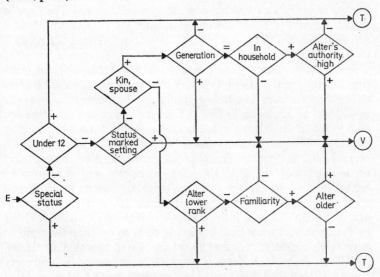

Fig. 3.1. Nineteenth-Century Russian Address
(From Ervin-Tripp, 1971, p. 25. Reproduced by permission of Mouton & Co.)

One criterion for its evaluation, however, is whether it predicts usage. From the model one would expect any member of the nineteenth-century Russian gentry speaking to a child under 12 to use (T), whereas whenever an older person was spoken to, in a status marked setting, the term (V) should be used.[1] Special statuses refer to the Tsar and God, while status marked settings are settings such as courts and duels.

Fig. 3.1 gives us an important guide to the conventions within a segment of nineteenth-century Russian society concerning T/V usage in much the same sense that there are conventions within our own society concerning the form of address used when meeting people. The diagram is misleading, however, if it suggests that contexts can always be established independently of pronoun usage, for pronoun usage itself can crystallise the nature of the context for participants. Friedrich illustrates this when, with reference to Tolstoy's *Resurrection*, he notes how switching or maintenance of pronoun would imply 'special hostility, affection or ambivalence' (1966, p. 244). The point can also be made in the context of Lermontov's novel *A Hero of our Time*. In the final scene, an aristocratic young lieutenant unexpectedly meets at an inn an older captain, a man with whom he had served on an isolated outpost in the Caucasus. The captain rushes forward, but the lieutenant speaks first: 'How delighted I am, dear Maxim Maximych! Well how are *vy*?' 'But . . . *ty* . . . *vy*?' muttered the old man with tears in his eyes.

So in many contexts the conventions will hold, while in other contexts the use of (T) or (V) may enable participants themselves to make inferences about the nature of the context, a person's intentions, or whatever. In fact in Chapter 2 we saw that Frake felt able to make the inference that his informant did not want to enter into close discussion of his illness on the basis of the term which was selected to describe Frake's sore. Predicting whether one term or another will be used on such occasions will therefore be hazardous, but in many ways these occasions are of more interest to the sociologist. Where (T) or (V) are used in a predictable manner, in certain contexts, little or no additional information is carried by the terms and some linguists would want to describe the word as not having meaning.[2] Thus when we say 'Good Morning' or 'Hello' or 'Hi' to each other, these utterances, in the main, do not carry much meaning, but their omission, or use in some kind of unusual circumstances, can signify a great deal – anything from a flirtatious gesture to a humorous remark. In the first case I am thinking of a man or woman acknowledging each other for the first time, in the second the case of two people meeting each other for the third or fourth time in an office corridor in the space of half an hour.

The alternation rules provided by Friedrichs/Ervin-Tripp give us a guide to conventional usage, but where such usage takes place

our interest in the (T) or (V) in question is likely to be limited in
that the item will not significantly inform or add to the meaning
of the stretch of talk. Where the item does add meaning – where, for
example, participants can make inferences about the intentions of
others on the basis of its selection – the alternation rules will be
least useful as predictive devices and they will not resolve for us,
of course, the question of what kind of meaning the use of these
items introduces into the conversation. I have already indicated that
a large number of possibilities are open on this score; in fact, several
are contained in Friedrich's analysis. The selection of (T) or (V)
could be used, for example, to accomplish a snub, to indicate
intimacy or special hostility, or to engage in a political act. The
omission of these kinds of consideration, however, is characteristic
of much sociolinguistic work. Blom and Gumperz (1972), in an
interesting and detailed account of dialect variation in a town in
northern Norway, give us much information about the sorts of
situations, topics and relationships which lead their respondents to
employ Ranamål or the more standard Bokmål. They include
analyses of recorded conversations, but frequently we are not provided with the procedures which allow them to make conclusions
about the meaning that is attached to alternation patterns between
these dialects. Take for example the following: 'Only in a few
instances when A began telling local anecdotes did he lapse into
Ranamål. (R) forms were introduced as metaphorical switches into
what were basically (B) utterances to provide local colour, indicate
humour, etc.' (1972, p. 431.) But clearly the interspersal of (R)
forms did not always carry this meaning, just as an 'inappropriate'
use of *vy* in Russian did not always carry the implication of a snub.
What sort of knowledge therefore is being drawn on to arrive at
such descriptions?

Rather than attempt to give a comprehensive account of sociolinguistic rules, I want to pursue the issue I have just raised by
asking whether it is possible to identify such speech acts as snubs,
accusations and promises, by providing a set of rules for their
execution which would allow an analyst to decide what sort of
speech act he is confronted with.

Those who have tackled this issue have generally begun by
drawing a distinction between the meaning of the words contained
in an utterance and how the words are being used, between the act
of saying something and the act we perform *in* saying something,
between what is said and what is done, or, in Austin's terms,
between the locutionary and illocutionary force of an utterance.

Austin argued (1962) that most acts of speaking are at the same time both locutionary and illocutionary acts, but that it nevertheless made sense analytically to distinguish these features. Thus the utterance, 'I will come at five o'clock' carries a certain locutionary meaning in that we recognise it as a grammatically appropriate sentence and one which employs items of vocabulary which are well known to us, but when uttered in specific contexts it may be heard as having the force of a warning, an appeal, a promise or whatever. This kind of distinction is probably well known to sociological field workers interested in investigating things like complaints in prisons or threats in the home, and it may well be that it is the lack of any close connection between the overt grammar and semantics of utterances, and the force of utterances, which has led them to eschew any systematic and detailed examination of the force of utterances in linguistic terms. The absence of this level of analysis in much naturalistic inquiry may indicate, rightly, the complexity of the cultural competence being drawn upon in such matters.

In the elaboration of Austin's ideas by writers such as Strawson (1964) and Searle (1969), special emphasis has been placed on the notion of *intention*, and intention became crucial through the influential work of Grice (1957). Grice held that to speak of the non-natural meaning[3] of an utterance by S one needs to assume that: (i) S intends to produce, by uttering x, a response (r) in an audience A; (ii) S intends that A shall recognise S's intentions; (iii) S intends that this recognition by A will function as at least part of his reason for response r. Austin raised the point that to perform an illocutionary act was to bring about in some way the meaning and force of a locution, and if one elaborates this idea of 'uptake' in Grice's terms then it is possible to see the illocutionary force as deriving in a significant way from the speaker transmitting a specific kind of intention to the person being addressed. For writers like Strawson and Searle, to understand the force of an utterance, and what sort of illocutionary utterance it is, is very much bound up with recognising the audience-directed intention, and with recognising it as intending to be recognised.

Before turning to the application of these ideas, it is necessary to explicate a further characteristic of Austin's notion of illocutionary acts, namely their conventional nature. By this Austin does not mean that they conform to specific linguistic rules, for example rules as to how plurals are to be marked in a given language. These rules are relevant to the locutionary meaning of a speech act, not to the illocutionary force. The latter derives from the standardised and conventional relation which is being drawn on in any speech act such that the meaning of the items, under these circumstances, is conventionally associated with producing particular effects on hearers of the act. The utterance of the word 'Guilty' for example, by the foreman of a jury, at the proper moment, constitutes the act of bringing in a verdict, the force of the speech act deriving from the location of the act within a set of legal procedures and conventions. The argument implies that gestures such as raising one's finger for silence may also have illocutionary force, an implication acknowledged by Austin, and it is for this reason that the specific term 'speech act' rather than illocutionary act has been used to refer to illocutionary acts taking a verbal form.

On the basis of these ideas Searle attempts to provide sets of conditions which model our competence as hearers to recognise a number of speech acts.[4] The conditions which he supplies for the speech act of promising are intended to be both necessary and sufficient for a promise to have been made, though he is careful to qualify this argument in a number of ways. He makes it clear, for example, that he is dealing with what he sees as 'the centre of the concept of promising' and ignoring 'marginal, fringe and partially defective promises' (1969, p. 55). He argues that this will involve him in idealising the notion of promising, a consequence which he finds acceptable in that 'without abstraction and idealisation there is no systematisation' (p. 56). Moreover, he is not arguing that all promises which we recognise as promises fulfil the necessary and sufficient conditions which he outlines. He writes: '. . . a condition may indeed be intrinsic to the notion of the act in question and not satisfied in a given case, and yet the act will have been performed nonetheless. In such cases I say the act was "defective" '. (1969, p. 54.) So the conditions below are conditions which, when taken together, are necessary and sufficient for a full-blown promise to have taken place (see Searle, 1969, pp. 57–61):

If S utters a sentence T in the presence of a hearer H then, in the literal utterance of T, S sincerely and non-defectively promises that p to H if and only if the following conditions obtain:

(I) *Normal input and output conditions obtain* (e.g. utterances are serious [rather than, say, play acting] and literal [rather than metaphorical or sarcastic]).

(II) *S expresses the proposition that p, in the utterance of T* (i.e. something is promised, p).

(III) *In expressing that p, S predicates a future act A of S* (i.e. S must promise to do or not do something now or in the future).

(IV) *H would prefer S's doing A to his not doing A, and S believes H would prefer his doing A to his not doing A.*

(v) *It is not obvious to both S and H that S will do A in the normal course of events.*

(VI) *S intends to do A* (for Searle this also implies that S feels able to do A).

(VII) *S intends that the utterance of T will place him under an obligation to do A* (a central condition for Searle because if S could demonstrate that he did not have this intention '. . . he can prove that the utterance was not a promise' [p. 60]).

(VIII) *S intends to produce in H the knowledge (k) that the utterance of T is to count as placing S under an obligation to do A. S intends to produce K by means of the recognition of S's intention, and he intends this intention to be recognised by means of H's knowledge of the meaning of T.* (This rule enables the intention of S in (vii) to be achieved by making the utterance and clearly draws on the notions of convention and intention which originate in the writing of Austin and Grice.)[5]

(IX) *The semantical rules of the dialect spoken by S and H are such that T is correctly and sincerely uttered if, and only if, conditions (i) – (viii) obtain.*

Searle leaves somewhat ambiguous the way in which we as hearers of a promise, or as analysts of texts in which speech acts such as promising are taking place, use these conditions to identify promises. It is clear that he is *not* saying that whenever someone uses the words 'I promise . . .' we check up in one way or another that all the conditions are fulfilled in order to see if it can be treated as a full-blown promise. When a speaker says, 'I promise to do A', and we hear it as a full-blown promise, Searle would argue that one of the reasons we hear it that way is that we hear the person as intending to do A (i.e. fulfilling condition (vi)). We may have no direct evidence concerning this matter, but if evidence were to emerge subsequently which suggested that the person did not intend to do A, then we could legitimately accuse the person of promising insincerely. In some cases, then, the conditions are not checked as to their presence or absence at the time of hearing the promise. But it is clear that in many cases the conditions are checkable and are checked at this time, and I want to consider whether these conditions will allow us as analysts to extract from conversation full-blown promises in the way suggested by Searle's analysis.[6]

In general, I would agree with Searle that to make a promise involves committing oneself to certain conventions within a society. There is no doubt, for example, that if I make a promise and it turns out that I did not intend to keep it in the first place, then this will be an accountable matter, and one for which I may be taken to task. The problem for us as analysts of conversation, however, is whether the conditions suggested by Searle allow us to identify in any specific case whether a verbal act was a full-blown promise, and I shall argue that they do not and that, furthermore, if one were to employ Searle's conditions as a way of identifying promises one would rarely, if ever, come across a promise.

My first point is that to apply several of these conditions in a specific context is a matter which would require supplementing the conditions with further conditions/rules which would allow us as analysts to decide whether or not the original condition applied. Take condition (i). It implies a competence to distinguish between promises which are part of a play or meant in jest from those which are serious and real. This distinction has been a common one in recent philosophical writing, but clearly it is not a hard and fast one. In order to decide the matter in a specific case, therefore, one would have to develop criteria for distinguishing between contexts – criteria for saying that this is a certain kind of situation. In the later part of this chapter I want to question the extent to which the use of such criteria can be distinguished from an interpretative competence in using the criteria. Furthermore, as with the use of *ty* and *vy*, there will undoubtedly be cases where the use of the words 'I promise . . .' itself creates the context which is supposed to warrant the way in which the promise is heard. In the following, artificial, example child B's promise can be heard not only as a real promise but as marking a transformation of the context in which the speech takes place from one characterised by humour to one of seriousness:

Child A (laughing): I'll give you all my soldiers if you give me yours.
Child B (laughing): I'll give you *one* if you give me *all* yours.
Child A: But if you gave me those I promise I'd give you any you wanted.

In these cases, then, it is unclear how we can identify the context independently of the utterance in which we are interested. Where we may think that it is possible to identify the context in an independent way, and where in practical affairs we are forced to make such decisions, the problematic nature of contexts becomes evident. In many cases court proceedings are required to decide on the nature of promises and on whether they were made in jest or with serious intent, so that even if we were to decide on a set of criteria for distinguishing contexts the application of those criteria will be a tricky business.

I want to develop a second line of argument by looking at condition (vi), which states that when a person is heard as making a promise the person is heard as being able to carry out the promise if the promise is to be a non-defective one, or what I call a full-blown promise. Imagine a scene in which a soldier is about to separate from his sweetheart at the outbreak of a war. The soldier promises to marry her after the war. If the sweetheart hears this as a promise does she accept, unconditionally, that the soldier is able to carry out the promise? Suppose my wife promises to buy me a pair of trousers on a shopping expedition to a nearby town. Surely I do not hear her as claiming to be able to carry out that promise under all circumstances. If we were to hear promises in such a way it would imply that at the time of hearing a promise no justification or excuse would be thought relevant or legitimate for an inability to fulfil condition (vi). Now this might bear some resemblance to the way in which young children hear promises, but what one learns in the course of childhood, and as a result of disappointment, is that such statements are not thought of as unconditional by adult speakers and hearers. Searle is right in claiming that if it transpires that a person is heard as not being able to keep his promise this may be a ground on which to reject or comment on his promise as being an inadequate one. His model is misleading, however, if it suggests that when we as adults hear promises we hear them as unconditionally fulfilling condition (vi). But if we accept this it leaves unexplicated the process by which hearers decide that *some* circumstances relevant to the non-fulfilment of condition (vi) bring into question whether a promise has been made, while others do not. Any adequate set of conditions for promising would clearly have to incorporate such information.

Searle might respond to the soldier–sweetheart example in the following way. He might say that it is, for his purposes, a defective promise in that the hearer, the sweetheart, does not hear condition (vi) as being fulfilled. It is not therefore an example of the full-blown promises which his rules are designed to represent. I would make two points about this argument. The first has been mentioned already and need no further elaboration: condition (vi) is not fulfilled in the vast majority of cases, therefore if promising were a matter of fulfilling these conditions we would rarely, if ever, hear a promise. The second is more of a methodological point. To assess the force of Searle's reply one needs some guide as to the members of the class of full-blown promises. Without this it is quite possible for Searle to exclude various counter-examples to his argument as simply not fulfilling the requirements of his set of conditions, and we are left in the position of not knowing what kinds of counter-examples could bring into question the adequacy of his analysis. There are various difficulties of this kind tied up with Searle's insistence on using his criterion of 'defectiveness' simply to re-work examples to make them consistent with his own analysis.

Searle does *not* purport to provide the necessary and sufficient conditions of all promises, only those which he calls non-defective ones, and which I have referred to as full-blown promises. Searle would admit, therefore, that what we sometimes recognise as promises do not satisfy all his conditions, and to this extent his analysis is only useful for identifying a sub-class of promises. I have argued that Searle gives us little idea of the members of this sub-class, and that problems associated with the form of these conditions and their application would either require us to pay further attention to the context in which an utterance is made, or leave us unable to hear as promises many utterances which we do hear as adequate promises.[7] Lest these difficulties are construed as simply having relevance to Searle's inquiries, I now want to illustrate some of them more briefly in connection with some rules for commands developed by Labov.

Labov argues (1972) that if a command is to be heard as a valid command then, where A is the speaker and B the hearer, B must believe that A believes that:

1 X needs to be done.
2 B has the ability to do X.
3 B has the obligation to do X.
4 A has the right to tell B to do X.

Notice here how the social distribution of rights and privileges becomes an explicit and formal part of the knowledge required to identify valid commands (in condition 4). Thus, in his example below, Labov argues that we hear Stanley's utterance as a refusal

(and as signifying an invalid command) because it raises doubts
about the applicability of condition 4, given that Stanley is the
president of the boys in the gang whereas Rel is only one of the
officers:

> *Rel:*   Shut up please!
> *Stanley:* ... 'ey, you telling' *me*?

But the way in which we as hearers make use of such features as
conditions 1–4 relies heavily on our contextual knowledge of particular cases. Take the following example:

> *Mother:* Take your clothes upstairs.
> *Child:* I'm just putting these toys away in here.

In some circumstances we might hear the child's utterance as a
refusal, but clearly not always so. It might depend on how many
toys the child still had left to put away, the degree of urgency
attached to the circumstances (e.g. whether a visitor was expected)
which the child might be expected to be aware of, and so on. The
mother *may*, like us as hearers, decide that the child's utterance is
a refusal, and her subsequent utterance, for example, may indicate
that she sees the child as questioning condition 4 and her rights on
this sort of occasion. But she *may*, like us as hearers, decide otherwise. Given that the hearing is contextually indeterminate in this
sense, one could argue that to hear, say, condition 4 as being
doubted or brought into question is always in some sense an
occasioned accomplishment.

Both Searle and Labov have made explicit reference to members'
knowledge about the rights and obligations of various participants
in speech settings, and while such knowledge is for them only part
of the knowledge involved in making and evaluating speech acts, it
is clearly a point at which we, as sociologists, might be expected to
make some strong contribution in the light of our long standing
interest in social norms and the distribution of statuses within a
society. In order to use Labov's analysis, for example, the sociologist might be able to specify norms which will help us as hearers
to hear Stanley's utterance as questioning the rights of Rel to
give him orders in this situation. The sociological norm specification
which is required then is of the form: 'In a class of settings S with
participants of status A and B, there is a norm to the effect that
only A has the right to make a certain class of utterances u.' If

Stanley is taken as an instance of A, Rel's command as an instance of u, and Rel as an instance of B, then the norm specification might help us arrive at the kind of hearing of Stanley's utterance indicated by Labov.

Sociological discussions of norms do not generally tend to be cast in this form. There are discussions of how people are socialised into being competent norm users, of the circumstances which lead to the emergence of norms, of the ways in which people evade norms; and the discussions are littered with conceptual distinctions such as those between formal and informal norms, preferred and basic rules, norms as expectancies and norms as behaviour. But somehow we want to stop short of the kind of formal specification of a norm which has been given above. One good reason for this is the recognition by several writers that norms and their applicability on particular occasions are to some extent indeterminate and negotiable. This can be documented in a number of different areas of sociological investigation. In the case of mental health, for example, Stanton and Schwartz (1954), in their classic study of a mental hospital, noted how rules seemed frequently to become relaxed, how certain people constituted 'special cases' in terms of a rule's application; and these findings have been extended along similar lines by Strauss et al. (1963) and Rushing (1964), who emphasise how the rights and duties of particular statuses are negotiable features rather than rigidly norm-governed.

At a theoretical level the point has recently been acknowledged by Brittan, who argues that: '. . . in interaction, the rules are open to revision provided they do not completely violate the logical structure of the situation'. (1973, p. 129). There is an important ambiguity in Brittan's use of the word 'revision' here: it might imply that members actually go about *changing* the rules in any given situation, or it might imply that the 'fit' between circumstances and rule is indeterminate in some respect. The latter interpretation is more interesting from our point of view, since it may help us to understand why sociologists have eschewed the kind of formalisation set out a little earlier; and it is this interpretation which informs some symbolic interactionist writing on the subject. Turner, for example, writes that:

. . . in most situations what the role-player expects from the relevant other on the basis of the latter's role is not likely to be a specific action but some behaviour which will be susceptible to interpretation as directed toward the ends associated with the other role, expressive of the sentiment which dominates the role in question, or as consistent with the values attached to the role. [1962, p. 33]

Cicourel (1973) also stresses how the use of norms requires an interpretative competence to recognise settings as ones to which the norms pertain.

Once we accept that interpretative processes are relevant to the application of rules in specific settings, a number of further issues are raised. Let me illustrate some of these with an example which Wieder uses in his discussion of the inmate code in a rehabilitation agency for drug-addicts on prison parole (1974). One of the residents said to a member of staff, 'You know I can't organise the baseball team.' Wieder argues that this utterance could be heard in a number of different ways. For example, it might be heard as, 'I don't know enough about baseball, or organising, to organise the baseball team.' Or, if it had been uttered by a *specific* resident with further *specific* grounds for disqualification from organising the game, the utterance could be heard as invoking an acknowledgment on the part of the hearer of those further grounds. When Wieder heard the remark, however, he heard it as an instance of the resident's code, more particularly of the rule 'Show your loyalty to the residents'. He heard the utterance as saying something like, 'You know that if I organised the baseball team I would be seen as doing favours for the staff, I would be seen as a "kiss ass", which would bring into doubt my loyalty to the other residents.' Further, Wieder is not saying that his knowledge of the code would allow him to hear the utterance in this way in any context whatsoever. He argues that his hearing of the utterance is bound up with the specific context in which it occurs; with who was saying it, where, and when; and on the relationship between hearer and speaker. The norm, 'Show your loyalty to the residents' cannot be said in any meaningful way to predict the hearing of such utterances, because the hearing depends on the additional significance of these various contextual features. More importantly though, the identification of an utterance as an instance of the code is intrinsically bound up with knowledge of the code and of how to use the code. The particular utterance does not gain its code relevance independently of our use of the code; the code itself is employed as an interpretative device by hearers to make sense of utterances. The traditional distinction, therefore, between inmate norms and behaviour which is governed by these norms is a misleading one in that the norms do not, in themselves,

tell us what behaviour to expect; and because instances of behaviour characteristic of the norms can only be seen as such by
using the norms themselves as interpretative devices.

Let us return to the norm specification required to supplement
Labov's analysis:

> In setting S with participants of status A and B, there is a norm
> to the effect that only A has the right to make a certain class of
> utterances u.

Wieder's work seems to cast doubt, for example, on whether it is
meaningful to distinguish as independent elements for analytic
purposes a norm and a class of utterances u. In identifying Stanley's
utterance as a refusal the norm does not, in some independent way,
allow us to say that the norm is being broken here. Rather, the
norm is being interpreted as being relevant to the situation; it is
being used as an invocable feature, by us as hearers and by Stanley.
The implicit claim that this invocation is a warranted one is thus
open to dispute on grounds such as the relevance of the rule to this
particular relationship in these particular circumstances.

In concluding this chapter I want first to re-state the formulation
problem which I outlined in Chapter 1. The problem was whether
or not we could extract a reading, a formulation of a conversation,
in some relatively unequivocal way; and the strategy in Chapters 2
and 3 has been to see whether the meaning of a term or an utterance can be defined according to a set of features or rules. When
a person wants to describe a scene or a person, there are usually
a number of correct descriptions which might be used; and one aim
of sociolinguistic analysis has been to specify a set of contextual
constraints which account for the alternation pattern between the
linguistic items concerned. I have argued that such analysis does not
take us far, however, since the use of items such as *ty* and *vy* has
most import for the meaning of sentences when used in some
non-standard way; and that in these circumstances sociolinguistic
analysis does not provide us with any procedures by which their
significance can be extracted in a systematic manner. Furthermore,
there is a class of cases with regard to both *ty–vy* use and promises,
where the use of the item in question can itself be heard as marking
a transformation of the context in which the utterance is made;
a context which, according to these models, is supposed to warrant
the reading of the item in question. The question, then, became one
of deciding whether a speech act such as promising, or at least a

sub-class of promises, could be accounted for in terms of a set of rules. A number of arguments were used here, but the general conclusion was that any set of conditions would require supplementing with further conditions, and an analogy was drawn with more recent discussions of norms in sociology which stress the interpretative competence which is used in deciding such matters as whether a particular instance is an instance of any norm. Lastly, Wieder's work was drawn on in order to question the analytic distinction between a norm and an instance of behaviour in accordance with that norm. I have tried to stress throughout that these arguments do not imply that for hearers there is great uncertainty as to what they hear, or, for example, that the conventions to which the sociolinguistic analysis or componential analysis draw attention are not powerful, real sorts of things. Indeed I see them as *more* powerful in some ways than the models suggest that have been reviewed. This general point is crucial in understanding the ethnomethodological strategy for analysing talk, and I shall now go on to expound the main features of this strategy.

4

Ethnomethodology

The ethnomethodological position is founded on the paradox at which I hinted at the end of Chapter 3. On the one hand, the meaning of words and utterances is indexical, bound up with and occasioned by the particular contexts in which words are uttered. Moreover the meaning of words is imprecise in any strict sense, by which I mean that there are various difficulties which are encountered in the arguments of those who claim that the meaning of words and utterances can be represented by a set of criterial features or a set of rules. Talk, then, is a form of *glossing*, by which ethnomethodologists mean that the analysis of meaning is never exhausted by a simple analysis of the words uttered. Yet on the other side of the paradox we have the fact that talk is experienced by participants as an ordered phenomenon. The ethnomethodological strategy is to explicate the *methods* by which glosses (talk) are produced and heard as ordered phenomena. The emphasis is on the study of meaning as an ordered accomplishment and the aim of ethnomethodologists is to inform us of the nature of that accomplishment.[1] In this chapter I shall examine these arguments in more detail by looking closely at an example of ethnomethodological work and by examining a number of criteria by which such work may be assessed. First of all, however, I want to indicate in more detail the way in which writers such as Garfinkel see the meaning of words and utterances as being tied to contexts of use, as indexical, and as being a form of glossing.

Take the following pair of utterances:[2]

A: Isn't it nice that there's such a crowd of you in the office.
B: You're asking us to leave, not telling us to leave, right?

If we hear B's utterance as an attempt to *formulate* seriously what is in A's utterance, we might want to ask B how he arrived at this particular formulation, to ask what it was that A said which justified such a formulation and to which the formulation referred. An interview with B on this subject might run something as follows:

I(nterviewer): When a person makes an utterance of the kind that A did we do not always formulate it in this way. Sometimes we might formulate it as an expression of approval that, for example, an otherwise empty room is for once filled up. What led you then to formulate it in your way?

B: Well, A has the right to tell people to leave as it is his office, and from the way he said it he seemed to me to be hinting strongly that we might leave.

I: But don't you also have rights in the room, rights to be treated as guests, therefore what led you to think that, in this case, A was asserting his rights over and against your rights?

B: I'm not sure. I guess it would tie in with the way in which he said it and the sort of person that A is. He is the sort of person you might expect to make that kind of remark.

I: Are you saying that *whenever* A makes this sort of statement you treat it as a request to leave?

B: Well, no. As you said at the beginning, he can express approval in this way also. So I suppose I am driven back to the immediate context of the utterance to justify my formulation.

I: Well, what was it about the way he said it which made you think he was asking you to leave rather than, say, joking?

B: Well, it was obviously a serious remark.

I: Obvious in what way?

B: Well, he didn't smile at all when he said it, and it didn't relate to anything that had been said before in a joking way, or an approving way for that matter, so what other way could you take it?

I: Well, we don't always smile when we make jokes, and I am not at all clear what you mean when you say that A's remark 'didn't relate to anything'.

B: Well, we were talking about gardening when he suddenly came across and made the remark without apparently paying any regard to what we were saying.

I: Perhaps he hadn't heard what you were saying and was just

trying to be sociable and make conversation.
[etc.]

B clearly finds it difficult to say precisely what it was about the
situation which led to his formulation that A was asking them to
leave. The application of such expressions as 'asking us to leave,
not telling us to leave' seems to be an indeterminate kind of process,
and the fact that it is indeterminate is what can allow A to make a
rejoinder to B's utterance which may be heard as faulting B in a
number of ways. For example A might reply:

No, you're the guests and you only leave when you wish.
or   I didn't mean that at all.
or   Don't be so touchy.
or   I don't want *you* to leave, I was referring to the others.

Thus Garfinkel and Sacks write:

. . . the very resources of natural language assure that doing
formulating is itself for members a routine source of complaints,
faults, troubles, and recommended remedies, *essentially*.
[1970, p. 353, their emphasis]

The word 'essentially' may seem unnecessary, but around it hinges
an important issue, for Garfinkel and Sacks are arguing that the
utterances of natural language users are essentially indexical glosses,
that it is not possible to specify the meaning of an expression independently of a particular occasion of its use, nor, even within a
specific context, to specify the meaning of expressions in a determinate manner. This is suggested in our conversation between
I and B above, but Garfinkel has tried to demonstrate this in a
number of ways.[3] For example, he has tried to show that the meaning of an utterance may change as a conversation proceeds, that
subsequent utterances constitute a new context in the light of which
reinterpretations of the meaning of prior utterances are made. In
other studies he has examined closely the coding behaviour of investigators who try to classify various aspects of documents and
verbal reports according to prearranged categories and schedules.
He has found that the implementation of such schedules requires
various 'ad hocing' practices such as the use of 'etcetera' and 'unless' clauses. Thus in order to use schedules sensibly, he found
coders including cases as members of a category even when such

cases according to formal criteria and prior agreement fell outside the range of application of that category; and excluding cases which, though eligible, did not seem to warrant inclusion. Such 'ad hocing' procedures, he argues, are an essential part of any classification exercise which purports to handle language phenomena, and they testify to the essential incompleteness and opaqueness of a rule-based semantics.

The problem which Garfinkel raises then is that if meaning is bound up with occasions of use, and if even then utterances are glosses which do not relate in any strictly rule-bound way to the contexts in which they occur, how do we go about analysing natural language phenomena? Going back to our earlier example, if B cannot tell us *precisely* what it was about A and A's utterance which led him to formulate it as 'asking him to leave', and if a hearing of A's expression is bound very much to that particular occasion, what sort of analysis are we to carry out on such expressions as students of language? The ethnomethodological solution is to change the analytic focus from what is being talked about to an investigation of the ways in which, for example, people decide on what is being talked about, the *methods* employed to remedy the essential indexicality and opaqueness of speech. Garfinkel writes:

> 'Shared agreement' refers to various social methods for accomplishing the member's recognition that something was said-according-to-a-rule and not the demonstrable matching of substantive matters. The appropriate image of a common understanding is therefore an operation rather than a common intersection of overlapping sets.[4]
> [1967, p. 30]

Going back to our example, Garfinkel would probably agree with the reaction of most readers to the interview between I and B, that it is an unnecessary and uninteresting task to expect B to be able to provide the information that I was after. Nevertheless we hear the original pair of utterances as ordered, sensible talk, so the ethnomethodological question would be to ask what sort of methodology we employ to hear the talk in this way, to raise questions about the methodology which informs interpretative processes.

One method which has been extensively discussed by Garfinkel, the documentary method of interpretation, has already been referred to in Chapter 3, in our discussion of Wieder's work on the inmate code. This method is a very general one and refers to the practice of treating an appearance (a word, an utterance) as standing for a presupposed underlying pattern, while underlying patterns are in turn derived from specific appearances. The example I used earlier was the way in which Wieder heard the utterance 'You know I can't organise the baseball team' as gaining its occasioned meaning from his hearing the utterance as an instance of the inmate code. Garfinkel himself illustrates the methodology in a contrived situation in which students were allowed to ask questions concerning their personal problems of a person they were told was a trainee student counsellor (1967, Chapter 3). Students were only allowed to ask questions which required yes/no answers, and the answers were given by the counsellor from another room on a random basis. The students appeared to treat the counsellor's yes/no answers as sensible, and in his comments on the results Garfinkel stresses how the students seemed concerned to search for a pattern in terms of which a particular 'yes' or 'no' could be given significance. In cases where 'incongruous' or 'contradictory' replies were given, for example, students were able to interpret the incongruities as being the result of the adviser having learnt more about them between the two replies, or as having a 'deeper' and unifying meaning behind them associated with the kind of advice the adviser was attempting to give. In looking for the pattern behind the yes/no answers students also employed cultural knowledge about counsellors, the sorts of things counsellors might be expected to do, and so on. In much the same way one might hold that in our earlier mock interview between I and B, B's first reply to I employs the background knowledge which B has of A in order to render what for B was the meaning of A's utterance. The connection is, of course, a defeasible connection, just as the connection which Wieder heard between the inmate's utterance and the code is defeasible. In both cases it is possible for the other party to provide 'good grounds' for faulting such a connection.

In the light of my arguments in previous chapters I can see little objection to this as a general characterisation of the way meaning is built up in interaction. Indeed the documentary method of interpretation is a logical implication of the theory of meaning which Garfinkel adheres to. If one cannot specify in a rule-bound way what are to be the criteria for utterances to be heard, say, as promises or snubs, if there is always to be some interplay between specific contexts of use and the hearing of such utterances, then clearly the interplay between contexts[5] and expressions will be central to any analysis of the methodologies which are employed to make particular hearings of speech. In the hands of Garfinkel and Wieder the documentary method is chiefly of interest as an illustration of the central theoretical tenets of ethnomethodology; in Garfinkel's case this is accomplished by contrived experiment, in Wieder's case through close analysis of the way in which he himself came to attach meaning to particular expressions. This does not, however, take us much nearer to any analytic specification of the *kinds* of methodology used by members to remedy indexicality, and in order to assess the nature of such methodologies, and problems of their evaluation, I now turn to an examination of an example of ethnomethodological writing.

I shall examine Turner's attempt (forthcoming), in the context of the following conversation between a psychiatrist and a new patient, to provide us with what he calls the 'machinery' to hear one of the utterances in a particular way. The opening utterances of the interviewer are as follows: [6]

(Psychiatrist)	T1	Will you sit there? What brings you here?
(Patient)	P2	Everything's wrong. I get so irritable, depressed. Just everything and everybody gets on my nerves.
	T3	Yeah.
	P3	I don't feel like talking, right now.
	T4	You don't? Do you sometimes?
	P4	'T's the trouble, I get too wound up. 'F I get started I'm all right.
	T5	Yeah? Well, perhaps you will.
	P5	May I smoke?
	T6	Sure. What do you do?
	P6	I'm a nurse, but my husband won't let me work.
	T7	How old are you?
	P7	Thirty-one, this December.
	T8	What do you mean, he won't let you work? (Clears throat.)
	P8	Well, (clears throat) for instance, I'm supposed to do some relief duty two weeks this month, next month, September. And he makes it so miserable for me that I'm in a constant stew . . .

The particular utterance we are interested in is T7, for Turner's argument is that this utterance can be heard as a comment on a complaint, the complaint being contained in P6. More precisely: 'T's remark (T7) can be heard as saying, in effect, "Are you a child, that you pass on that responsibility to others?" or "Surely you're old enough to be responsible for your own decisions?" ' (op. cit, p. 29).[7] Now this hearing of T7 is not the hearing which the original investigators of this conversation arrived at, nor is it the one which at first glance P appears to arrive at; but for the moment I will leave this issue aside, since the primary task of the ethnomethodologist is to provide us with the methodology/machinery by which *this* particular hearing is arrived at. Let us also assume that P6 is heard as being a complaint,[8] as well as a response to the question contained in T6. The machinery then has to provide us with a way in which we can hear the question *How old are you?* as a comment on utterance P6, the complaint. As I understand it, Turner's argument runs as follows:[9]

1 A complaint (c) can be considered the first part of an 'adjacency pair' such that to utter a complaint sets up an expectation for hearers that the utterance following (c) is to be heard as a member of a limited set (s). There are two classes in this set in the case of complaints:
   (a) negatives – in which the response is heard as an attempt to diminish the complaint in some way, e.g. 'Well, what do you expect?'
   (b) positives – in which the response is heard as accepting and sympathising with the complaint, e.g. 'Yeah, I know just how you feel.'
2 Questions can be heard as members of (s) as well as non-questions (i.e. questions such as T7 can serve a variety of functions, one of which may be to diminish complaints).
3 Conventionally within the society, for any class of members, there is a class of activities which can be invoked as *permissibles* (i.e. activities which require the permission of others to perform) and a class of persons which can be invoked as *responsibles* (i.e. persons empowered to give such permission). Conversely there is for a class of members a class of activities which can be invoked as *non-permissibles* and a class of persons as *non-responsibles* (i.e. the hearing of utterance P6 as a complaint seems to trade on this conventional knowledge; work in our society is not the sort of

thing which, for adults, other people such as husbands are conventionally seen as having rights over).

4 If in a particular instance a complaint (c) by person (p) is set up so as to trade on p's non-permissibles being treated as permissible by a person f who is conventionally a non-responsible, then one way of diminishing the complaint is to notice that p is not a member of that class of person for whom such activities are permissibles.[10]

Such attempts at formalisation, while crude by linguistic standards, tend to put many sociological readers off, so let me try to describe more lucidly how the machinery works. The complaint P6 emerges as a complaint partly because it highlights a state of affairs in which P's husband is held to be unjustifiably controlling his wife's right to work; which is to say that the wife is trading on our conventional common-sense knowledge of social structures in some way (point 3 above). The complaint itself sets up an expectation that T7 will either be a diminisher or a sympathiser; that T7 is likely to be faulting or accepting the complaint in some way (point 1 above). The fact that T7 is a question is basically irrelevant here, since questions can function as diminishers or sympathisers just as well as other types of utterance (point 2 above). We can hear T7 as diminishing the complaint in the way that Turner hears it, if we can hear the question as noticing that the patient P is old enough for her work activities not to be controlled by her husband (point 4 above).

First, I shall attempt to clarify just what sorts of procedures/ rules are being employed in this machinery. The main point here is that it does not seem to do them justice to describe them as either optional or obligatory rules. Take the adjacency pair; complaint plus answer. The rule that we should expect the next utterance after a complaint to be some sort of answer is clearly optional in the sense that answers do not always follow complaints, and where this happens it cannot always be attributed to a mishearing of the original complaint. But in a sense the rule is more than optional in that if an answer to the complaint is *not* provided then this can become a noticeable matter in the subsequent talk. A person can be heard as ignoring a complaint, a feature which is provided for by this machinery, and to propose that a complaint has been ignored is an accountable, justifiable sort of thing to do by virtue of its reference to this rule for orderly talk. Put in a slightly different way, the rule may be invoked, in the absence of an answer, as a rule which was binding in some sense in these circumstances. A second point to note here is that rather different *kinds* of rules make up the machinery that Turner provides. We can represent two of them formally as follows:

(i) $C - - - - \rightarrow (P + R)$

(ii) $C \rightsquigarrow A_2C$

Here C is a complaint (e.g. P6); P and R are permissibles and responsibles; A_2C is the second part of the adjacency pair, the first part of which is a complaint; $- - - - \rightarrow$ denotes 'can be heard as'; $\rightsquigarrow$ denotes 'sets up an expectation for the hearing of the *next* utterance'. Whereas (i) is a rule concerning the way in which we are to hear an utterance, (ii) is a rule concerning the connection between two utterances, P6 and T7; (i) has a single utterance function, the second an inter-utterance function.

The general aims of such work need to be carefully documented as they are clearly central to any consideration of its success. At this point we limit ourselves to the aims avowed by the group of ethnomethodologists centring around Sacks, Schegloff and Turner. For this group the aim is to extract general conversational structures, such as adjacency pairs, which can be seen to be operating in a variety of social contexts; structures which have general application. Sacks, Jefferson and Schegloff write:

> Since conversation can accommodate a wide range of situations, interactions in which persons in varieties of identities and varieties of groups of identities are operating, be sensitive to the various combinations, and be capable of dealing with a change in situation within a situation, there must be some formal apparatus which is itself context-free, which by virtue of its context-freeness – its unsituatedness – can in any local instance of its operation, be sensitive to, and exhibit its sensitivity to, various of the parameters of social reality in that local context.
> [forthcoming, p. 5]

Turner also espouses such aims, and they seem to be necessary aims if any kind of general knowledge is to emerge from ethnomethodological work, if analysis is to go beyond the documentation of how orderliness is achieved in any given instance of talk. Turner makes a number of more specific claims as to the nature of his analysis, and I shall next examine these claims as a way of pinning down some of the problematic features of carrying out ethno-methodological work. The following claims are made by Turner:[11]

1 His analysis is susceptible to being shown as incorrect or inadequate.
2 It is possible to replicate these structures so as to account for talk in other settings.
3 The structures can be used to generate new instances of acceptable talk.

Turner does not explicate these criteria formally, nor does he formally apply them to his own analysis. By claim 1, however, I understand him to mean that the machinery which he provides is full enough and explicit enough to retrieve the hearing of 'How old are you?' which he has proposed. If we follow his rules we should be able to do so without confusion, and the rules should allow us to hear the utterances in this way rather than some other way, to hear 'How old are you?' as a diminisher of a complaint and not, say, as a straightforward questionnaire-type question concerning the patient's age.

I want to deal first with the question of whether the rules can be followed unambiguously. To follow the rules we have to make a procedural agreement with the analyst that the hearing of at least one utterance can be taken as unexplicated. This is a purely logical point in order to avoid problems to do with regress. If it is not acceptable to make the assumption that P6 can be heard as a complaint, then the machinery for *that* utterance also has to be provided, so that logically we have to provide the machinery for at least all prior talk in any exchange. I take it that the assumption of 'hear one utterance at least as unexplicated' is a necessary assumption for most analytic work. More seriously, to follow the rules without confusion in Turner's example we have to be able to hear adult female work as an instance of a non-permissible, an action which does not require the permission of others. The extent to which this piece of machinery can be used unproblematically depends on how problematic the relation between 'adult female work' and the class of 'non-permissibles' is *in this instance*, that is in the instance of our hearing P6 as a complaint. I take this as an unproblematic connection *in this case*; indeed, our very acceptance of P6 as a complaint involves us in making this kind of connection. Third, I want to focus on whether we can use the machinery for diminishing the complaint without confusion. The specific machinery in the case of

P6–T7 was to notice that P was not a member of that class of persons for whom such activities as work were permissibles. Now using this machinery, and without knowing what the next utterance (T7) was, we might have expected the next utterance to be something like 'But surely you're of an age to decide that sort of thing for yourself.' As I understand it, however, the point of the machinery is not to predict the next utterance in this sense: rather we are supposed to use the machinery in the following way – follow all the procedures in the machinery, and if the next utterance can be heard in the way that the machinery provides for, then hear it that way. We have to ask ourselves whether, using the machinery's instructions, we hear 'How old are you?' as meaning for us as hearers, something like 'Surely you're old enough to be responsible for your own decisions.' At this point the issue of the adequacy of the machinery becomes inseparable from our ability to use the machinery without confusion, and I now turn to the more complex question of adequacy.

Turner argues that the fact that the analysis can be found to be empirically incorrect is one of its virtues, and earlier I took incorrect here to mean not full enough to allow us to hear 'How old are you?' in the appropriate way. It is as well to make explicit here a distinction between an *incorrect* and an *inadequate* set of machinery, since I shall discuss the analysis under both of these headings. An incorrect analysis would be a machinery which led us to hear 'How old are you?' as a different type of utterance from that which was intended. In the case we are dealing with, for example, an incorrect machinery might lead us to hear 'How old are you?' as a questionnaire-type question concerning the age of the nurse. An inadequate analysis would be a machinery which allowed us to hear 'How old are you?' as, say, attempting to diminish a complaint, but did not lead us to expect an utterance which diminishes the complaint in the particular way provided for by the reading. In this particular case, I would argue that there seem to be no grounds for holding the analysis to be incorrect, but there may be grounds for considering it inadequate.

The problem I find with the correctness criterion is that of conceiving circumstances in which the machinery could be found to be incorrect. The problem here seems to be that a variety of readings can always be made of any utterance; in fact so many that it is difficult to conceive of an utterance which could *not* be heard in the way provided for by the set of instructions in the machinery. My impression is that in this instance 'How old are you?' for example, could not be heard as doing a certain number of things (e.g. promising), but that it could be heard as doing a wide variety of other things – casting doubt, advising, complaining, expressing indignation, expressing interest in the nurse's medical history and bodily state, and so on. Thus if a machinery for hearing 'How old are you?' as a promise were constructed, the machinery would be incorrect in that it cannot make the utterance, in this instance, hearable as a promise. But if it is not hearable as a promise no analyst would involve himself in trying to provide for that reading of the utterance, so even where the criterion of correctness could be applied it would not be applied in practice. For these reasons I think that the criterion of correctness is of much less significance than the criterion of adequacy in the evaluation of ethnomethodological work.

The notion of adequacy is a slippery one, since what is to be taken as adequate machinery depends to a great extent on the purposes of the analyst and on how delicate his analysis is intended to be. In order to illustrate these points I shall try to provide some grounds on which, for certain purposes, Turner's analysis could be found to be inadequate. His machinery provides for us to expect a next utterance as one which notices that the nurse is not a member of that class of persons for whom work is an activity requiring permission. Turner clearly thinks of this class in terms of the contrast between adults and children, children being conventionally required to obtain permission from others on various matters. But other groups in our society are also conventionally in this relation of dependence upon others, prisoners for example. If Turner's aim, therefore, was to provide us with a set of instructions which prepared us to hear T7 in the precise way that he originally heard it, he needs to provide us with further machinery which will select hearing $T7_1$ rather than hearing $T7_2$ below:

P6	I'm a nurse, but my husband won't let me work.	P6	I'm a nurse, but my husband won't let me work.
T7	How old are you?	T7	How old are you?
($T7_1$	'Surely you're old enough to be responsible for your own decisions')	($T7_2$	'Surely you're not a prisoner, are you?')

It should be emphasised that this is not necessarily a criticism of Turner's analysis, but rather highlights the way in which the adequacy of any machinery, like any methodology, must always be considered in relation to the analyst's purposes in carrying out the investigation, and the level of abstraction at which he is working. Thus at one level of analysis it would follow from what I have said that the simple specification of the adjacency pair (complaint + sympathiser/diminisher) would be adequate if Turner's aim were simply to provide a procedure for hearing T7 as the second part of the adjacency pair.

I noted earlier that Turner also makes other claims as regards his analysis; and the first that I want to examine is the claim that parts of this machinery can be used to help account for the orderly hearing of talk in other settings. This claim is, of course, central if ethnomethodologists are to build up some general body of knowledge concerning these matters and, as has been stressed, this is an explicit aim of at least one group of ethnomethodologists. The usefulness of adjacency pairs has been documented in a number of other analyses, and various types have been distinguished such as question–answer, greeting–greeting, and offer–acceptance/refusal. The ordering effect of a question–answer pair may be illustrated most vividly by considering conversation sequences in meetings[12] in which an answer to an initial question may be delayed for twenty or more utterances, yet the answer, if and when it comes, may be readily recognised as an answer to the earlier question:

Q: Well, how do you think we should tackle this?
(20 utterances)
A: Well then, I think we should . . .

Although few analyses have employed the machinery of permissibles and responsibles, there is clearly no logical or theoretical reason why the machinery should not have more general application. Two further points need stressing here, however. First, I have argued that the rules incorporated in the machinery have a peculiar status in that they are not strictly optional or obligatory rules; and since they are not strictly obligatory they will not be generative in the ways in which many formal linguistic rules are generative. Second, in any specific investigation of talk further, supplementary machinery might be required in order to develop a more delicate and adequate analysis, though the extent to which this need be the case would depend on the aims of the investigator.

More problematic is Turner's third and last claim that this specific analysis should generate new instances of acceptable talk. This seems to be true, but true in an uninteresting way. When a machinery is provided it is assumed that the person using the machinery is a culturally competent member, so that when I read an instruction 'notice some aspect of a married woman which indicates that she has a right to determine whether or not she works', I cannot help but generate new acceptable talk. By definition, then, *any* use of the machinery must in some sense generate acceptable talk.

I now turn to consider the relation of the analyst's machinery, and the utterance it makes hearable, to the surrounding text, and particularly to the utterances which follow. I have argued that for certain purposes Turner's machinery may be taken as adequate for the hearing of 'How old are you?' as 'Surely you're old enough to be responsible for your own decisions?' in this instance. We can also ask, however, whether in this instance it is just this reading which is the relevant one for which to provide a machinery *if our aim is to carry out an overall analysis of the dialogue*. The last qualifying clause is, of course, crucial because if we are not interested, say, in the relation of 'How old are you?' to subsequent utterances and the surrounding text then the question of additional readings becomes less significant. But if we are interested, one criterion in deciding which readings to provide for must be whether such readings are a necessary part of the machinery for the hearing of subsequent utterances. Put more generally, the readings we choose to account for must be connected in some way with our reading of subsequent utterances.

Turner implicitly recognises the force of this argument in a footnote which is worth quoting in full:

> It would appear from P7 that P does not in fact get the drift of T7 (as argued here), but does in fact treat it as a 'questionnaire-type' question . . . (this) does not of course stand as evidence of anything other than P's hearing of that utterance. The argument advanced in this paper gives grounds for finding P to have engaged in a mis-hearing. Further, T's subsequent, *What do you mean, he won't let you work?* then figures not as a 'delayed' response to P6 . . . but as a reformulation of *How old are you?* [op. cit., p. 16]

Turner's argument, then, is that the nurse's response 'Thirty-one, this December' (P7) may be taken as a mishearing of the reading of 'How old are you?' which Turner has been attempting to account for. Now clearly it need not be a mishearing. We might hear the nurse as responding in a rather cold, minimal way to what she considers an aggressive and unnecessary attempt on the part of the psychiatrist to fault her complaint; and presumably we could provide a machinery for such a hearing. Let us suppose that we do hear 'Thirty-one, this December' as based on a mishearing of 'How old are you?' This implies that we may have to provide more than one machinery for the hearing of 'How old are you?'; one for its hearing as a questionnaire question and one as a diminisher of a complaint. Furthermore, the *selection* between such machineries by a next speaker (the nurse in this case) may itself become a noticeable feature for a subsequent speaker (the psychiatrist) if the nurse can be heard as intentionally selecting one machinery rather than another. For example, if the psychiatrist had said at T8 'Why are you avoiding my question?', the machinery to produce a hearing of *this* question might involve reference to selection procedures between the hearing of 'How old are you?' as a questionnaire question and as a diminisher of a complaint. The machinery at this point for the hearing of 'How old are you?' begins to look a bit cumbersome; but it is a necessary machinery if ethnomethodology is to handle the phenomena of mishearings and misunderstandings, and it should be borne in mind that we could probably describe the machinery in a much more abbreviated and elegant form through the notational conventions of symbolic logic.[13]

After spending so much time on the machinery for one utterance I find myself slipping into the view that because the machinery works well for this utterance then it is likely that the hearing which Turner initially made of the utterance is the most adequate hearing. This is clearly a kind of 'reflexivity trap' in which we, as analysts, use the analysis as a way of deciding on a *correct* hearing of a conversation. Once stated in this way it must be clear that to take such a step would be quite inconsistent with the ethnomethodological strategy, though it is a step which, of course, many conventional sociologists would feel justified in taking. A similar, but slightly different, way of claiming that a specific machinery and reading were the most adequate would be to argue that there is some sort of evidence in the text which suggests that members themselves are orienting to this machinery. This raises the interesting general question as to what relationship there is between the analyst's hearing and machinery, and those of participants in the actual conversation being studied. The logic of their theoretical position would seem to commit ethnomethodologists to making a radical distinction between an analyst's hearing and a member's hearing.

If it is always possible for members to have heard the piece in some different way, then it is always possible for the analyst's machinery and hearing to have little bearing on the methods employed by coparticipants. In the Turner paper which I have been examining, the machinery for the hearing of 'How old are you?' which Turner provides would have little bearing on the procedures used by coparticipants if the psychiatrist heard P6 as simply stating that the nurse was not working at the moment, and the nurse heard T7 as a questionnaire-type question seeking routine information about her age. Some parts of the machineries for the two hearings might be similar, but the similarity need only be coincidental.

But some ethnomethodologists are prepared to make stronger claims for their machinery. Schegloff and Sacks argue that a machinery for ordering turn-taking among speakers in a conversation is a solution which members develop for the problem of maintaining two basic features of conversation: only one party speaks at a time and speaker change recurs. They write:

> These basic features of conversation, the problem of achieving their co-occurrence, and the turn-taking machinery addressed to the solution of that problem are intended, in this account, not as analyst's constructs, but as descriptions of the orientations of conversationalists in producing proper conversation.
> [1973, p. 292]

They are careful to note that such a claim requires thorough documentation. One way of doing this would be to show that events which would count as violations of the turn-taking machinery would also be 'noticed events' for participants in the conversation. Thus Schegloff and Sacks suggest that:

> The noticeability of silence reflects an orientation by conversationalists to the 'at least . . . one at a time' feature; the feature must be oriented to by conversationalists, and not merely be an analytic construct, if conversationalists do accomplish and report the noticing.
> [1973, p. 293]

This argument seems to imply that if two alternative machineries for turn-taking were developed, one way of deciding on the more adequate one would be to look for evidence which suggested that members actually orient more to one than to the other. Schegloff and Sacks are concerned here with general conversational machineries, and they are saying that in some circumstances evidence as to the psychological relevance of their machinery can be adduced.[14] In many cases, however, such evidence will not be present; there is no special evidence in the text, for example, which persuades me that Turner's machinery rather than some alternative machinery is being used by the nurse and the psychiatrist. Yet there is clearly a concern that at the more abstract and general level of analysis the conversational structures being extracted are structures which are in some way oriented to by members, and for which relevant evidence can be provided.

The ethnomethodologists I have been dealing with in this chapter[15] attempt to account for the ways in which stretches of talk are heard as ordered phenomena. They attempt to do this by providing sets of instructions, rules and machineries (I have tended to use these terms interchangeably) which are at the same time general and yet applicable to specific instances of talk. These general machineries are not seen as invariant rules; they are machineries which may be used, and whose absence may be noticed in the ordering of talk, but their generality reflects the fact that we order talk in general ways, and the analyst's aim is to track down these general ways as they affect particular conversations. I have spent some time explicating these views, because much criticism of ethnomethodolgical work contains misplaced assumptions as to the nature of their endeavour. In later chapters I shall express some misgivings as to whether this work is likely to be the only productive strategy for dealing with naturally occurring talk. So far I have concentrated on the ways in which we might begin to evaluate ethnomethodological work. The explicitness of the machinery, the analyst's purposes, the correctness and adequacy of the machinery, the evidence that members are orienting to such a machinery, have all been cited as relevant to such an evaluation. In general these issues receive little overt attention in ethnomethodological work and it seems fairly clear that the machineries will need to become more formalised; first, in order that these complex analyses can be presented more elegantly, and second, because the relations between various parts of the machinery need to be stated more formally so that the nature of their interdependence can be made more explicit. Now, however, I want to turn to the question of whether the debates of the last four chapters have any bearing on sociological work which has been traditionally concerned with analysing speech, though I shall return to a discussion of some aspects of ethnomethodology in Chapter 6.

5

Language and Social Class: Vocabularies of Motive

In this chapter I shall examine some of the issues tackled in earlier chapters in the context of two traditional research areas within sociology which have concerned themselves in a direct and explicit way with the analysis of talk. I should stress that I am not attempting to provide an overview of research findings in these areas, nor an inventory of all the methodological problems involved in doing such work. My strategy, as in earlier chapters, will be to raise a limited number of theoretical and methodological issues which are related to the controversy which constitutes the theme of the book, to raise them in the context of specific pieces of research, but at the same time to make apparent their wider implications.

I

One area in which most sociology students will have thought about language concerns the way in which children's home backgrounds lead them to use speech in different ways. It is the language and social class issue, an issue which, in recent years, has tended to focus around the age group 2–8, and, in this country at least, has been kept very much alive in the research and theoretical work of Bernstein. Any empirical investigation of such issues immediately requires the classification of speech in one form or another. In regulative contexts, for example, where a mother can be heard as trying to persuade a child to do something (or not do something), analysts are required to distinguish such speech acts as imperatives / commands, for Bernstein claims that these are more characteristic of speech use in working class homes and that they also constrain the subsequent development of dialogue.[1]

In natural discourse the classification of speech acts as, for instance, commands, is problematic both for children and investigators. It is the fact that the force and sense of a parental statement is often ambiguous which leads children into perennial interaction problems with adults over such matters. One of their difficulties, for example, is to decide with what seriousness of intent and purpose a particular command is made by a parent, and if they interpret it too lightly they stand to be accused of 'being cheeky' or to be questioned as to their comprehension of the utterance concerned – 'Did you hear what I said?'[2] I take it that most sociological investigators would be interested in the meaning of utterances for participants themselves (in this case children's hearings of parental statements), so a minimal requirement must be that our classification scheme does no grave injustice to children's definition of events. In classifying an utterance as a command, therefore, we have to make an inference from the context and the child's behaviour in order to decide whether the parental utterance merits 'command' status. Moreover, we usually have to do this within a framework of coding rules (i.e. our own rules as to what are to count as commands), so that these also have to be judged as fulfilled or not fulfilled in each case.

One soon comes across the problem that the coding rules are inadequate as a way of retrieving what are intuitively felt to be genuine commands; and that what appear on the surface as genuine commands can function in different or ambiguous ways. Utterances such as 'Leave it alone', 'Shut up' and 'Put it on' are not invariably heard as commands. Imagine a mother doing a jigsaw with her child; both are absorbed, and the mother says to the child in a non-threatening intonation 'Put that piece there.'[3] Imagine a mother who, laughing at being tickled by her child, and continuing to laugh, says 'Oh no, don't touch me any more.' Would we want to classify these statements as commands, suggestions, requests, jokes, or something else? Going back to my first point, it is fairly obvious that almost any kind of utterance can function as a command. Imagine the effect, in some households, of a father calling up the stairs 'What did I tell you?' when he has heard sounds from the children after they are supposed to be asleep. The problem which an analyst faces, then, is how to decide on the statements which are to count as commands, and how to describe for other analysts the procedure he has adopted in arriving at such decisions.

One strategy adopted by researchers is to provide a number of
general criteria for the classification of the speech act in question,
and to leave it flexible and open to the coder's interpretation as to
whether particular utterances should be classified in one way or the
other. This is not just a strategy of naturalistic investigators but also
of those who rely on more structured data-gathering techniques.
Cook-Gumperz, for example, was concerned with analysing the
responses of mothers in an interviewing situation to such questions
as:

> What would you say or do if (the child) brought you a bunch of
> flowers and you found out he/she had got them from a neigh-
> bour's garden?
> *or*
> Supposing you thought it was time (the child) went to bed, but
> he/she started to cry because he/she wanted to watch something
> on TV. What would you say?

She goes on to write that:

> . . . categories . . . were *descriptive* rather than precisely *defined*,
> each category in the coding handbook had a theoretical descrip-
> tion and examples of the behaviour to be coded under that
> category. These definitions of the categories specify the necessary
> conditions but not the sufficient conditions, which allows some
> interpretative space for the coders . . . in the last analysis a coding
> system is successful if it does not violate the commonsense know-
> ledge of the coders. It is this shared commonsense knowledge,
> not the scientist's 'metalanguage', which provides the substratum
> of consensus without which any form of shared data interpreta-
> tion becomes more difficult, if not impossible.
> [1973, pp. 218–29]

An investigator constructing this type of coding manual writes
a set of instructions which are intended to guide and limit in some
way, though not to eliminate, the operation of common-sense
procedures; if they were eliminated there would be no coding problem, no room for judgement, no *problem* of reliability.

I want to note first of all that this procedure conceals, in effect,
the basis upon which coding decisions are being made, thus raising
various questions as to whether two different investigators can ever
employ the same measure in the same way. High levels of reliability

are not just produced by coding instructions plus common-sense knowledge such that any person with common-sense, who also understood the instructions, would code similarly to the original coders. This reliability is more a result of the experiences built up in 'training sessions' and the discussion of 'problematic cases'. These experiences provide coders with vital information as to how to *use* the sets of instructions with which they are provided, and from my own experience with similarly complex schedules it is extremely difficult to disentangle this process from that in which any new coder comes to learn the various rules and procedures of the instructions themselves, their internal relationship, priority rules and so on. Unfortunately these are difficult arguments to document in any precise way.[4] The best reports of coding procedures usually give such information as who the coders were, what sort of experience they had of the population being studied, the efforts made to ensure high reliability, the nature and results of reliability tests, and how ambiguous items were dealt with. The acquisition and use of knowledge in coder training has not come in for much sociological attention, in spite of the increasing concern of organisational analysis with problems associated with rule use. In fact the predominant model of coding error is one which views it as due, for example, to insufficient briefing or inadequate knowledge of instructions – in other words as the result of information deficit – rather than to the nature of the coding task itself. The acquisition of an inexplicit interpretative capacity to use the coding instructions is acknowledged by writers such as Cook-Gumperz, but this capacity is an unknown from the point of view of others who use the same coding schedules, and for readers of such work who are concerned to check the accuracy of coding procedures.[5]

A further point follows directly from my argument in previous chapters.[6] In coding a response an investigator is, in effect, formulating an utterance, but there is no way of being sure of the formulation, so that formulations, as Garfinkel and Sacks (1970) stress, are *essentially* liable to being undercut and faulted. Things are not even as straightforward as this in dealing with replies to questions in structured interviews, for here the coder is attempting to formulate respondents' formulations concerning their own likely behaviour. Bearing in mind that each formulation is liable to be undercut in a number of ways it seems to me highly speculative what bearing, if any, the results of such investigations have on the behaviour of subjects. Moreover, this is before we bring to bear any of the more conventional criticisms of such techniques; their demand effects, the tendency of mothers to distort their answers more towards what they consider to be the norm of childbearing, and so on.

A more complex and detailed strategy for handling and classifying the talk of children from different social classes has been developed by another of Bernstein's coresearchers, Turner (1973). An analysis was made of role-play speech used by 5- and 7-year-old children when describing a set of four pictures which showed a sequence of events during which a boy broke a window with a ball. Role-play speech was defined as sequences in which the child quoted or reported people's speech when describing the story contained in the four pictures (e.g. 'The man said: "You're very naughty" '; or 'The man said that they were very naughty'). Turner provides a detailed 'meaning potential' analysis of this language of control ascribed by children to adults. This involves a sociological classification of this speech according to dimensions of meaning which are relevant for sociological purposes (i.e. the left hand side categories in Fig. 5.1) and formal linguistic definitions of these meaning options (i.e. on the extreme right hand side of Fig. 5.1). In Fig. 5.1 the full meaning potential analysis is only provided for rule-giving, and it is only in this case that all the sub-categories (numbered 1–8) can be given a formal linguistic description.[7]

Utterances are fed into the system from left to right, so that we first decide whether an utterance is imperative or positional, then go on to subdivide imperatives into commands and threats, and so on. Turner allows any one rule-giving utterance to be assigned to more than one coding category, and here are some examples provided by Turner of rule-giving, together with their code numbers:

Play football in your own garden. (1, 3, 7)
You shouldn't play right in front of the window. (2, 4, 8)
Don't play football out in the street. (1, 3, 8)
You musn't smash windows. (2, 6, 8)

The meaning potential analysis has a number of advantages from a sociological viewpoint. For example, whereas linguistic analysis is often something with which sociologists correlate their variables (e.g. sex and age variations in the incidence of subordinate clauses), here it is being used to supplement, and add precision to, the set of sociological distinctions. Turner himself notes a number of limitations which apply to his own work (op. cit., pp. 146–8), the nature of the interviewing situation being an obvious one, but I want to focus on whether or not the analysis resolves any of the problems

Fig. 5.1. *A Meaning Potential Analysis of Rule-Giving* (From Turner, 1973, pp. 153-60)

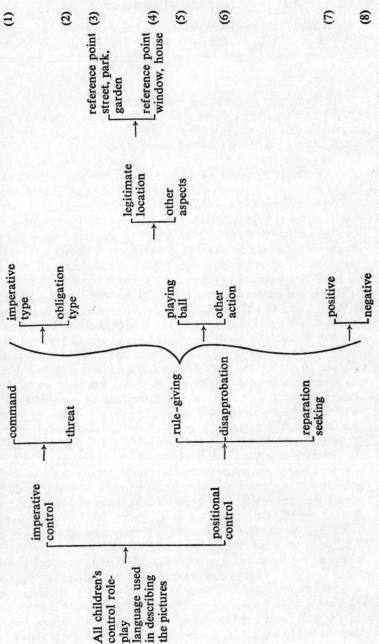

which have been mentioned concerning the classification and coding of utterances. Take the following three utterances, all of which were statements made by children in this context and classified by Turner in his analysis:

(i) Don't play football near our house again.
(ii) Don't you dare break that window again. Don't you dare do that again.
(iii) Don't you knock my window again.

To use Turner's scheme we have to decide, for example, whether the utterances are commands, threats, reparation-seeking, rule-giving or disapprobation.[8] To some extent this is misleading, since the analyst will have constructed his categories, at least partially, on the basis of his inspection of the corpus of responses, so he will be fairly sure that categories are pertinent to whatever data is at hand. *In this speech elicitation context* Turner's decision is that (i) is a rule giving statement (ii) an implicit threat and (iii) a command. The italicised phrase is, of course, crucial, because Turner would not, I think, claim that the utterances would be classifiable in this way in *any* context; and to make such a claim would clearly be incorrect. I selected examples (i), (ii) and (iii) above because I do not hear them as falling unproblematically into the categories to which Turner allocates them, in this context. To this extent there is likely to be a class of cases which are at least ambiguous as to their category membership, and for which the basis of categorisation is unclear to other analysts. There is a clear danger of resolving these ambiguities by recourse to the formal linguistic context of the utterance (i.e. categories on the right of Fig. 5.1), and of deciding, for example, that (ii) above is an implicit threat because it includes the word *dare*, which, on the basis of other threats in the analysis, may be a linguistic marker of threats. To do this, however, would be to use the model in an inappropriate way, since utterances are only fed in from left to right.

Even if we confine our remarks to those utterances which we hear and categorise in the same way as Turner, our categorisations are clearly defeasible categorisations. A child or an adult can always fault the categorisations that we made by virtue of the fact that the meaning of an utterance is never provided for by any specifiable and checkable set of conditions which would allow an analyst to be sure of, and able to defend, his reading of the piece. Nevertheless, Turner might want to argue that, while this may be the case, there is likely

to be sufficient consensus on the hearing of the set of utterances to
warrant his kind of categorisation exercise; and I would like to
examine this point in the context of my own research on parent–
child talk in the home, since I, like Turner, was concerned with
making a classification of utterances for various analytic purposes
(see Wootton, 1972). Suppose we confine our attention to parent's
regulative remarks. When classifying utterances I was concerned to
do it in a way which seemed to be consistent with how the child
seemed to be hearing the utterance, and with the hearing which I
made of the utterance as a culturally competent member. The usefulness of the enterprise depended upon assumptions being made as
to the equivalence of my reading and the child's reading, assumptions which were made in the absence of contrary evidence and in
the light of another culturally competent coworker reading utterances
in the same way. On the basis of such analysis I came to the conclusion, for example, that regulative utterances constituted a larger
proportion of parental speech in some homes than in others. My
position is, of course, that I cannot specify in any strictly rule-
defined way the class of utterances which I counted as regulative
remarks. I can give some guides to this, but in a number of cases
these guides would leave the basis of classification formally unexplicated. Moreover, as with Turner, any instance of categorisation
could be faulted by a hearer; a point which I shall illustrate in the
context of the following hypothetical example:

Mother: Put those biscuits back in the tin.
Child: But some are broken.
Mother: Put them all back.
Child: Why?

Any single categorisation of 'Put them all back' as a regulative
remark may well have little bearing on the meaning of that remark
for the child. In this case the utterance could simply be heard as an
information-giving statement which specifies in more detail the
nature of the task which the mother expects the child to perform.[9]
Notice here also the problems associated with using the child's last
utterance as evidence which can affirm our hearing of the mother's
'Put them all back.' To use the 'Why?' as evidence consistent with
our categorisation is to formulate the 'Why?' in some way. But the
formulation of 'Why?' is just as problematic as the formulation of
'Put them all back' which we are using it to warrant. Does 'Why?'
mean, for the hearer, 'Why must I *put* them back?' or 'Why must

I put them *all* back?' or 'Why are some biscuits broken?', or whatever? There is an obvious problem, then, with the argument that subsequent utterances can act as evidence for our selection of a formulation. Thus the investigator is left with formulations/categorisations of parental speech which may not capture the sense assigned to the utterance by the child, though he can fall back on a further argument, namely that his reading is the correct reading by virtue of his detailed knowledge of this family, of this sort of situation, of children and so on. Although there is clearly something in this argument, the problem is whether it constitutes adequate grounds in any specific case to exclude alternative formulations and categorisations. It is the classic participant observer argument, the sort of argument which, in Chapter 1, I expected Sudnow to put forward to defend his interpretation of the interview between the Public Defender and his client. I hope that by this stage it is clear that such an argument is problematic. In fact, the controversy to which this book is addressed centres around the problematic nature of this assumption.

It would be misleading to give the impression that the problems highlighted in the context of control sequences only have relevance to this aspect of the study of parent–child speech. The problems pervade all aspects of such study, and tend to become more evident in the context of natural dialogue which in many ways provides the most valid and satisfying data to deal with. A problem with which one is immediately confronted in analysing natural dialogue is the division of the stream of speech into contexts or topics of some kind. In looking through the literature on this subject I have found remarkably few guides to undertaking this enterprise. Those who have addressed the question have, rather worryingly, seen little that is problematic in the exercise. Having set up a number of general criteria for what they call 'episodes', Barker and Wright, for example, write that:

> . . . the required judgements usually are not analytical. The direction of the behaviour in relation to the new position and vice versa generally are immediately apprehended; the unity of the action in an episode is perceived almost as immediately as the unity of a visual form or an auditory pattern.
> [1955, p. 240]

In its focus on *how* meaning is ascribed to speech, the ways in which conversations are heard as orderly, as changing their topic and so on, ethnomethodology takes as its problem for investigation the way in which writers such as Barker and Wright (together with lay analysers of conversation) manage to organise conversations in such an orderly way. Their investigation of this phenomenon is not yet at a very advanced stage, but perhaps I can give a flavour of what form it might take through an example which Sacks provides of the way in which attention to topic and topical talk is exhibited. It involves analysing prior utterances in a conversation and linking subsequent talk with prior talk by means of using common class membership devices:

A: An' yer supposed to light it off yer boot.
            (laughter)
   If yer gonna be a politician, you better learn
   how to smoke cigars.
B: Yeah, that's an idea Rog.
C: I heard a very astounding thing about pipes last
   night.
[from Sacks, 1968]

Our hearing of the topic continuation in this sequence draws on what Sacks calls the 'co-class membership' of cigars and pipes, but it should be noted that not just any co-class member of cigar would necessarily make the talk hearable as a topic continuation and as exhibiting topic concern. For certain purposes cigars might be classed with diesel engines (e.g. as air polluters) but the co-class membership in this instance may not exhibit the same topic concern. So, as Sacks emphasises, the particular *selection* of co-class members is itself a way of exhibiting concern for the topic. The concern, then, is to show how conversation is organised, and exhibited as being organised, in such a way that members themselves, and we as hearers, can come to recognise such units of conversation as topics.

In this section I have tried to give some idea of the way in which the discussion of earlier chapters has a bearing on work concerning language and social class. The heart of the matter is the classification of speech and the retrieval of adequate accounts of the meaning of talk. I have suggested some problematic features of such investigation, particularly that the basis upon which such classifications are made is not explicated and open to replication by other analysts, and that the relation between the categorisation arrived at by the investigator and the sense extracted from an utterance by a hearer is uncertain. These kinds of difficulties, together with those outlined in

Chapters 1–3, would lead ethnomethodologists into a different set of research problems in the context of parent–child talk, and I have tried to give a preliminary, though abbreviated, idea of what one of these problems would be and how it might be tackled.

II

The idea of vocabularies of motive is at first sight an exciting one. It offers us, through the writings of Wright Mills and those who have pursued his line of thought, the idea not only of relating what people say about themselves to the social organisations of which they are a part, but also a sporting chance of extending a sociological bridgehead into one of the heartlands of classical psychology. On the one hand, motive vocabularies are seen as learned forms of behaviour in some way handed down to novitiates, the content of specific vocabularies being derived from the workings of wider social processes. Wright Mills, for example, saw a change in entrepreneurs' espoused motives from those of individual gain to those of public service and efficiency; and this change, he argued, is related to the internal development of capitalism from a *laisser-faire* to a monopolistic phase (Gerth and Mills, 1954, p. 118). At the same time, the notion raises possible connections with psychology. Mills certainly thought that in small pre-industrial villages vocabularies of motive and the 'real' motives of action would overlap, and the former '. . . will be used when alone and that they will be linked with impulse and emotion during the socialisation of psychic structure' (op. cit., p. 122.) In practice, however, the relation of motive vocabularies to 'real' motives is not an issue which has received much attention in the subsequent literature, partly because of the growing critical attention which has been paid to the notion of motive from within psychology itself.[10]

The dichotomy between 'real' motives and espoused motives needs modifying for our discussion to proceed, since it is clearly an over-simplified one. One point here is that espoused motives may also be broken down into those 'really' held by participants and those put on for the benefit of particular audiences. Hartung (1965), for example, claims that delinquents use aspects of conventional ideology (such as theories of cultural deprivation) as excuses for their mis-demeanours when dealing with agents of social control and, by implication, that such accounts would not necessarily be given to, say, their peers. Taylor justifies his inclusion of some interviews with sex offenders as part of the data for his study, on the grounds that they were '. . . of particular use in counteracting those accounts which were elicited under circumstances in which there may have been a pay-off for the offender who opted for particular descriptions.' (1972, p. 38.) These writers appear to recognise a distinction between espoused motives which are more or less genuinely held, and those presented to specific people for specific purposes.

A further consideration is that the presentation of a motive can be heard to be doing a number of different things. Mills, and subsequent writers, have taken the paradigm case of motive presentation to be occasions on which a person has failed in some way to do what was expected,[11] but motives can clearly be heard as constituting speech acts other than justification. Suppose I see my wife in the garden, struggling to dig something out of the ground, and on seeing me she says, 'I'm trying to clear this ground to plant some forget-me-not seeds.' It is possible to envisage circumstances in which I may hear that as a justification, but it is also possible that I may hear it as a request for my help, or simply as giving me information as to *what* is to be planted there, on the assumption that what she is doing is plain enough for anyone to see. Motive statements can then be part and parcel of a variety of speech acts and are not restricted in any clearcut way to specific kinds of context. Even in a context where a person is being taken to task for untoward behaviour, motives can be heard as doing a variety of things, for example as instances of excuses or justifications. This latter distinction received early attention from Austin (1961, Chapter 8), and was subsequently incorporated in an influential article by Scott and Lyman (1968). Justifications, they argue, are accounts in which the speaker accepts responsibility for the untoward act in question, but denies the pejorative quality; whereas excuses are accounts in which the pejorative quality is accepted but speaker responsibility is denied.

Peters makes a further relevant distinction when he notes that we do not conventionally consider all reasons for actions to be motives (op. cit., p. 35). He gives the example of explaining a person's action in terms of his considerateness or punctuality; and clearly, in certain circumstances, we might not hear such an explanation of a person's action as an explanation in terms of motives. More importantly for our present argument, we have to distinguish reports which we hear people making of their motives for action from reports which are heard as statements as to the inexplicability of their actions. The latter seem to be particularly characteristic of accidents, where people make remarks such as 'I just can't remember what made me turn round just at that moment.' But they are not only characteristic of accidents; people who climb mountains sometimes seem unclear about their reasons, but would hardly wish to describe their achievements as accidents.

I have distinguished, then, three problematic issues in connection with vocabularies of motive. First, an investigator may have to decide whether a set of motives is produced for a particular audience or whether these motives are genuinely held. Second, there is the problem of distinguishing between motives which function in different ways; for example as excuses or justifications. Third, any investigator may have to distinguish statements of motive from other statements of reasons for action, and from statements of non-reasons for action. I think that investigations of motive vocabularies draw upon at least one of the above distinctions, and I want to suggest some ways in which all of these distinctions are problematic. I shall discuss them roughly in the order that I have presented them here, and mainly in the context of a study of the motive vocabularies of sex offenders by Taylor (1972).

Some light can be shed on the problems involved in distinguishing valid from non-valid accounts by examining Taylor's enterprise of asking magistrates to make such a distinction. Twenty-six magistrates were asked to rate the credibility of a number of accounts given by specific categories of sex offenders. The accounts which the magistrates rated were selected by Taylor on the basis of a typology of such accounts which he developed. He distinguishes, for example, a general class of involuntaristic accounts such as 'breakdown of mental functioning' (e.g. (i) below) from voluntaristic accounts such as a refusal to accept normative constraints (e.g. (ii) below):

(i) I don't know why I do it – something just comes
over me – I have a blackout.
(ii) I'll do it to anybody – it's all a laugh to me.

Magistrates tended to rate the involuntaristic accounts as the more credible.

Magistrates, of course, routinely make decisions about the credibility of accounts, but they do it on the basis of the evidence available in individual cases. Furthermore, for the offender the decision that his account is voluntaristic or non-voluntaristic is highly consequential in that it may lead to a judgement of diminished responsibility and a different sentence. There are a number of general grounds upon which such a plea may be upheld in the criminal law – for example, drunkenness, automatism or abnormal states of consciousness not involving collapse, mental illness, physical compulsion by another person – and also, of course, possible claims which may be made in connection with *mens rea*, which will centre on the general knowledge and foresight which any reasonable person could have had in the circumstances.[12] Thus if a sex offender were to claim in a court of law that he had a blackout at the time the offence occurred, a crucial part of such a claim would be the documentation that he *was* suddenly deprived of all thought and that he could not be expected to have foreseen the occurrence of such a blackout in such circumstances. In some cases such accounts are upheld, in others rejected. When Taylor asks magistrates to make judgements of the credibility of accounts (independently of the evidence in the case) they are clearly not arriving at decisions in their customary way, and I take it that the information is supposed to tell us something about their attitudes or their past experiences with particular kinds of account. This information may be of interest, but its relation to any instance in which a magistrate makes an actual judgement is fundamentally opaque. By this I mean that in any such instance, given that we knew how that magistrate tended to rate the credibility of accounts (according to Taylor's measure), the bearing of this information on the actual judgement would be unclear from any analytic point of view.[13] This example illustrates some of the problems for sociologists in using experts to distinguish valid from non-valid accounts, particularly where the accounts are presented without the circumstantial evidence customarily used in order to decide such matters. Even where such evidence is provided, however, problems remain, and I want to go on to illustrate these in relation to the other questions which I raised earlier.

These questions were: how do we distinguish motives from other reasons for action; reasons from non-reasons; and motives which can be heard as doing different sorts of things? My argument will draw attention to some of the ways in which these distinctions may not be as clearcut as the literature implies, and to some of the methodological problems thereby posed for this body of work.

In examining the distinction between excuses and justifications, one central methodological question must be: can examples be unambiguously assigned to one class rather than the other? Austin makes a start towards clearing up the distinction by providing us with an example. X drops a tea-tray. X might say that this happened as an emotional storm was about to break out. X might say that the close attentions of a wasp led to the culinary disaster: 'In each case the defence, very soundly, insists on a fuller description of the event in its context; but the first is a justification, the second an excuse.' (1961, p. 176.) To claim that the impending emotional storm is a justification is to demonstrate that dropping the tray was a sensible, permissible sort of thing to do in the circumstances; in Scott and Lyman's terms it is to claim that the pejorative associations attached to dropping the tea-tray are offset in this instance by the pejorative qualities of an impending family row. There is no doubt that such a claim could be made, but there is equally no doubt that the claim may be treated by hearers as an excuse for X having lost his temper. In a similar manner *all* of the examples which Scott and Lyman provide of excuses and justifications could be heard as instances of the other category. For instance, they include the example of a Mexican youth who partially attributes his waywardness to the fact that the girl he truly loves is his half-sister, and thus unavailable to him for coitus or marriage: 'So, because of Antoni, I began to stay away from home. It was one of the main reasons I started to go on the bum, looking for trouble.' (1968, p. 120.) As sociologists, most of us assume that such matters are decidable, if only in some imperfect way, but clearly to decide such matters in either way in the examples I have just given is going to be controversial. If one of the Mexican's relations claimed (like Scott and Lyman) that his utterance was an excuse, he might retort that it was a justification and provide 'good grounds' for doing so. If we claim that we as analysts can put up a set of conditions which utterances must fulfil if they are to be counted as, say, excuses, this does still not resolve the issue in any satisfactory way, as I pointed out in Chapter 3 where I examined some attempts to provide for the meaning of utterances such as promises, according to a set of conditions. Austin's claim is more limited than the sociologist's. His argument is that it is possible, in the situation he constructs, to hear X's utterance as a justification. I suspect that my doubts about Austin's argument stem from a distinction which he himself makes elsewhere between intentional and purposeful actions. We might agree that the actions of gang members in lopping off the tops of young trees are intentional, but we may find difficulty in describing them as purposeful; and the notion of justification may be conventionally tied to the notion of purposeful action. In the case of the tea-tray dropper, we may hear his justification as one for reacting in *some* way to an impending emotional disturbance, but not for the purposeless action of dropping the tray.

In principle, the kinds of problems that have been found in

connection with the distinction between excuses and justifications apply equally to the further distinctions between non-reasons and reasons, reasons which are motives and those which are not. The problematic nature of the former distinction, for example, seems to be pertinent to Taylor's study of the accounts of sex offenders. The example which he provides of an offender appealing to 'a break-down in mental functioning' (a sub-category of involuntaristic accounts) runs as follows: 'I don't know why I do it – something just comes over me – I have a blackout.' The statement can be heard as similar to those made by many neurotic patients in psychiatric hospitals who cannot understand why they do the things they do, or have the feelings they have, but nevertheless provide various circumstances which they think may help a doctor to arrive at some diagnosis. The fact that fundamentally they cannot understand why they do the things they do, however, is attested by their attendance at a hospital and their concern to 'get to the bottom of the matter'. The question is then why the sex offender's account should constitute an involuntaristic account of the kind described by Taylor rather than a statement that the sex offender simply cannot account for the action which he has engaged in. These are not, of course, the only possible readings. Taylor himself suggests another when, as I have noted, he makes it clear that he thinks some of these accounts may be best understood not as genuine statements by the defendant as to what happened, but statements constructed for the benefit of the particular legal audience to which they are addressed.

The literature on vocabularies of motive seems fraught with these kinds of problems, but what distinguishes the field from the social class/language literature is that many of the most elementary questions concerning the way in which an investigator imputes meaning to utterances are unacknowledged, let alone remedied in conventional sociological ways. Consequently our discussion of the issues raised in this book cannot proceed as far in this area as it did in Section I. Those involved in such work must presumably find ways of demonstrating that the reading which they make of utterances is the correct reading, and to do this they will have to find ways of counteracting the kinds of criticism which I have made. The ethnomethodological view would be that from the point of view of the analyst investigating such utterances the pursuit of a correct reading, an adequate formulation, is a fruitless task; and the arguments relevant to that position are those which have been laid out in earlier chapters. One ethnomethodological strategy in con-

nection with motives might be to look at the way in which the
selection of motives exhibits and facilitates particular hearings of
utterances in much the same way that Schegloff (1972) poses the
question of how the selection of place names allows for further
inferential work on the part of a hearer. For example, if I write:
'What I like about that couple is that they are always loyal to each
other and never concerned to do each other down behind one
another's back,' if you hear 'the couple' not as a couple of police-
men but, say, as a married couple, the hearing may be selected in
some way by the motives which are provided in the utterance and
by the connections which we can conventionally make between
types of persons and types of motives. As I am not aware of any
published ethnomethodological analysis of motives, however, no
detailed account can be provided,[14] but in any case it would, of
course, be subject to the kinds of evaluation which I outlined in
Chapter 4.

6

Sociology, Language and Description

The problem which initiated the discussion in Chapter 1 was how to extract from a sequence of conversation the meaning of that conversation for participants. One solution was to examine the meaning of words by outlining the distinctive features which differentiate them from other words; for example those which distinguish the words *chair*, *sofa* and *stool*. Those linguists who approached the study of meaning in this way did not take as their aim the recovery of the full meaning of expressions, but rather an account which was sufficient for the purpose of communicating intelligibly. The success of such communication, they argued, is based in some way on our mutual acceptance of the distinctive features of the words which are used. The primary difficulty with this approach is that it distinguishes sharply between the meaning of words and what speakers and hearers *do* with words, so that linguists like Lyons prefer to discuss the meaning of words independently of particular speaker–hearer contexts. The upshot of omitting an analysis of context and of what people are doing with the words they are using, however, is that in many cases an analysis in terms of distinctive features would not allow us to understand in any adequate way what people are saying. Furthermore if, like Frake, we went to a different society and worked out the distinctive features of a set of terms, this would not allow us in any straightforward way to use these terms in the way that our informants do. The 'seeing' of a distinctive feature in any instance, for example, is problematic and negotiable, as Frake is at pains to stress in his account of the way in which the Subanun argue about diagnoses. The need to take context into account became particularly apparent when I noted that in some cases Frake felt able to make inferences about his informants' intentions on the basis of their selection of one descriptive term rather than another.

If we take seriously what participants are doing with words, then one way of deciding the meaning of expressions is to decide *what* participants are doing with them. In Chapter 3 I raised the question of whether we could decide this by setting up a number of conditions which would allow us to decide the meaning of expressions, conditions which made reference to contextual knowledge such as whether the speaker had the right to make such a statement (e.g. in the case of commands). If such conditions could be set up for a variety of speech acts then, presumably, we would be in a position at least to exclude various alternative readings of any particular speech sequence on the basis of the absence of the relevant supporting conditions for the speech acts concerned. Various difficulties were found with these arguments. For example, there were problems in deciding whether in any specific case the relevant conditions had or had not been fulfilled; and in the discussion of rules in sociology, and of attempts by sociologists to extract commands, threats and so on from ongoing conversation or parental reports, it has become clear that there is much reliance on the interpretative capacity of the investigator to supplement any conditions or set of rules laid down to guide his activity. In fact Wieder's work (1974) on the inmate code questioned the extent to which it was useful to think of these rules and sets of conditions as being independent in any genuine sense of the pieces of talk whose meaning they were intended to decide.

The other party to the controversy, ethnomethodology, builds on these various weaknesses and takes the view that the extraction of incorrigible formulations of the meaning of talk is an inappropriate strategy. For them, what we say is essentially liable to be heard in a variety of ways and, because of this looseness, any particular attribution of meaning is essentially liable to being undercut or faulted. This poses the problem of how it is that members of a society hear speech as an ordered, accountable phenomenon, when from an analytic point of view what they hear is always and essentially open to a variety of interpretations. The ethnomethodological task is to provide some account of the practical everyday reasoning procedures used by members to hear talk in particular ways, though I have noted that the extent to which members' reasoning procedures or analyst's reasoning procedures are being laid bare is to some extent ambiguous in ethnomethodological writing. Sacks, for example, certainly wants to claim that the general machinery which he provides for turn-taking in conversation can be heard in certain instances as being adopted by members themselves. In fact, he sees this as at least one criterion of the significance of the machinery. In other cases, such as Turner's analysis which I dealt with in Chapter 4, there seems to be more uncertainty as to whether members themselves could be heard as orienting to the machinery, and this question, together with various problems concerning the criterion of adequacy for the machineries, seem to me two areas within ethnomethodology which are in need of clarification.

At this stage I want to examine some of the implications of these arguments for some more central strands of sociological theory and methodology, and to discuss some issues concerning the general relationship between ethnomethodology and mainstream sociology. The first step in any serious investigation of the social world by a sociologist is that of description, in which equivalence classes are established. In the last ten years or so the features which we have considered worth describing, the features which have entered our conceptual schemes, have become increasingly cognitive; and some writers have gone so far as to claim that the increased saliency of cognitive variables constitutes the greatest single area of intellectual advance in modern social theory.[1] For example, symbolic interactionism, together with various strands of phenomenology, have assumed an increasingly central theoretical position, while in particular areas such as deviance analysis what are broadly known as interactionist approaches have constituted the central theme of debate in recent writing. Those philosophers of science more influenced by Wittgensteinian philosophy have been concerned to emphasise the significance and relevance of cognitive states and normative patterns in the explanation of conduct.[2] The intense concentration on the nature of human action came as something of a revelation for those of us who had tended to dismiss this as an area in which the abstract formalism of Parsons' work was destined to soak up the intellectual energies of interested students for some time to come.

The unifying theme of this change has been the concern for analysis in terms of meaning, and there has been a reinvention and relabelling of various traditional sociological ideas in such a way as to make more explicit the integral part of interpretative work in social processes. The words 'role conception' and 'typification', for example, are fundamentally similar in what they denote, but the latter term implies certain emergent and processual features in such a way as to leave more scope for the part played by individuals in negotiating and constructing the meaning of situations. What I want to argue is that while this concern with meaning has made a theoretical impact, in that it has changed the way in which many of us think about society and social processes, its empirical relevance has been obscure. One of the main reasons for this is that it has provided us with no satisfactory way of relating its suppositions concerning meaning to ongoing human conduct, particularly as exemplified in people's talk.

The problem can be documented fairly clearly in the influential writings of Schutz. His primary interest is the way in which social life is a construction of, and constituted by, the activities of people's minds. This constitutive activity clearly takes place through talk, but for Schutz talk itself is somewhat epiphenomenal and he devotes little space to explicit discussion of language and what people say. Where he does refer to it, it is mainly in terms of the vocabulary of a language. He writes, for example, that:

> By naming an experienced object, we are relating it by its typicality to pre-experienced things of similar typical structure, and we accept its open horizon referring to future experiences of the same type, which are therefore capable of being given the same name. To find a thing or event relevant enough to bestow a separate name upon it is again the outcome of the prevailing system of relevance.
> [1967, p. 285]

Objects exist in the outside world, but it is the way in which these objects are incorporated into systems of relevance and typification which is the starting point of Schutz's discussions; and the vocabulary of a language is a *reflection* of this process. While his stress on the 'open horizon' of words brings to mind the kind of indeterminacies stressed by ethnomethodologists, his emphasis in the last analysis is on the consensual properties of language and meaning, the reciprocity of perspectives as a condition of orderly interaction, the social distribution of common-sense shared knowledge, and so on. He recognises that aspects of this consensus are idealisations, that when I speak to someone, for example, I assume (unless in possession of counter-evidence) that he takes what I am meaning to say in much the same way that I mean it when saying it. But these idealisations constitute assumptions which act as stepping off points for other kinds of theoretical work, and as this work also stresses the shared reality and knowledge in everyday life his work has been criticised, rightly in my view, for overemphasising consensual aspects of meaning.[3]

In the writing of Schutz there is a tension between his emphasis on common meanings and the 'open horizon' of words and concepts. This represents in a way the tension which underlies the main theme of this book. For investigators of social life these issues become concrete in the analysis of that form of data which is routinely available to us, namely talk. If I am doing a study of complaints among prisoners and their interpretation by prison officers, one feature of interest may be the way in which prison officers have certain typifications of complaints. To say this is to say that prison officers hold conventional ideas about prisoners' complaints. But there are various problems concerning the way in which such typifications/conventions are used, and with identifying their presence in any instance. One of the problems which has preoccupied us in previous chapters is whether the use of the typification can be considered a rule-defined enterprise, whether the presence of certain features x, y, z in a prisoner's utterance leads that utterance, and other similar utterances, to be heard as complaints, or whether it is more useful to think of such features as criteria which may be used and which are fitted to situations by various kinds of defeasible reasoning procedures. The tension hinted at in the writing of Schutz, then, becomes an acute one in that one's style and strategy of investigation may depend upon the way in which such issues are resolved. Insofar as there is little explicit discussion of language and its properties in Schutz's work, he offers little guidance on these issues.

Similar problems occur in connection with symbolic interactionist writers. They attempt to overcome the problems associated with the over-determinate role model of social life by positing a situation of flux, in which the identification of the part one plays is subject to ongoing revision in the light of inferences made concerning the intentions and expectations of others in a situation. In Turner's formulation (1962) a role prepares us for a possible range of responses in a situation, but the crucial decisions are taken in the context itself where, in the light of all information available to us, we opt for one definition of the situation rather than another; the one which is most 'readily interpretable' (ibid., p. 34). Again, a tension is being recognised. Turner's emphasis on the 'loosely definable range of responses' and the 'interpretable' nature of action suggests that for the actor the act of fitting a description to a scene, even at one time within this scene, is an accomplishment of some kind. An accomplishment, presumably, in much the same way that our description of the scene as observers, concerned to retrieve actors' definitions, is an accomplishment. Yet symbolic interactionists have traditionally wanted either to give some generalised abstract account of what is involved in the nature of the accomplishment, or to go on to relate actors' definitions to other phenomena, such as actors' behaviour, in an attempt to account for that behaviour. A combination of the two is probably most frequent. That is to say, they usually provide us with a model of how interaction and role-taking can be seen to be working, and they present us with findings which are loosely based on this view of how interaction works, and usually purport to show how a definition of the situation influences conduct, or self-perception, or whatever. The model most favoured in their writing is a cognitive version of the behaviourist G. H. Mead's work (1967), which stresses the interaction between the 'I', the 'Me', and the 'Generalised Other' in two party exchanges; but in later writings such as Turner's (noted above) the model becomes more complex. The perception of the other person, for example, is seen more as a process of making hypothetical inferences and the interpretative dimensions of the model become more intricate. In spite of Mead's emphasis on the role of language, however, discussions of the negotiation of meaning rarely consider this in connection with properties of language. Mead writes: 'Language does not simply symbolise a situation or object which is already there in advance, it makes possible the existence or the appearance of the situation or object, for it is a part of the mechanism whereby the situation or object is created' (op. cit., p. 78). But if one takes these remarks in connection with those of Turner earlier, then there seems to be some recognition that the *way* in which language is constitutive of human activity is a problematic process. When we hear someone say something, the language used and the context in which it takes place make it interpretable as being an instance of X (e.g. a role, a purpose), but the implication seems to be that there is no tight, rule-based connection between these features in everyday life. In this sense, some symbolic interactionist writing seems consistent with the ethnomethodological position, though this is never worked out in too much detail, for the symbolic interactionists seem simply to recognise these tensions at the level of meaning without working out their implications at the level of talk. Because the tension is not recognised in their writing the typical questions which symbolic interactionists and ethnomethodologists seek to answer are quite different. For the former they are such questions as 'How are situations defined?' 'How do interactional rules emerge?' whereas for the latter they are 'By what procedures is the orderly sense of a scene produced?' 'By what procedures is the emergence of a rule made visible to others in an instance?'[4]

Both Schutz and the symbolic interactionists place language in a critical position in their analysis of meaning, but treat language itself as simply a medium of meaning, an intervening variable, without paying attention to the problems attached to the retrieval of meaning from people's talk. This lack of attention is reflected in the lack of sustained contact, in either of these bodies of work, with linguistic issues and with the discipline of linguistics. The Sapir-Whorf hypothesis has continued to be one point of connection, and we have also been prepared to accept the differentiation of animal and human behaviour in terms of language properties. Both of these issues are still important ones, but the bodies of knowledge now attached to each of them are complex and do not easily support the primitive sociological assumptions which have been drawn from them in the past. The supposed radical divide between human and animal communication, for example, has been subject to some modification in recent years.[5] It has been fairly convincingly demonstrated that chimpanzees can not only develop a vocabulary of words through the use of sign language, but that these words can also be combined in strings analogous to utterances and, more importantly, that the words and strings may be used in such a way that they are not tied to particular occasions and referents. Furthermore, there is some evidence that the structures underlying the strings may be used productively in the sense that a negative construction, for example, may be transposed from one string of words to another string of words by the chimpanzee itself, without its ever having seen the negative construction produced in the context of the second string of words. Even where we have traditional interests in such aspects of language study the issues are such that we need to become closely involved in various empirical debates concerning these matters, instead of using such work as a stepping-off point for making radical assumptions about, say, the distinctive features of human behaviour.

Many sociologists have *had* to come to grips with people's talk. Participant observers especially have had to construct descriptions of scenes and members' meanings, if only as a preliminary to the generalisations presented in research reports. Yet many of the problems confronted in this book do not at first glance seem of central significance in their work; they are not problems which receive much attention in the methodological literature concerning such enquiry. The lack of attention itself allows their work to be construed as consistent with more than one of the approaches which I outlined at the beginning of the chapter. It may be that participant observers agree with the Wittgensteinian analysis of language, and for this reason have eschewed attempts to relate linguistic categories to their conceptual schemes in any determinate way. For example, they may find young people 'sounding' each other, and may find that the notion of 'sounding' is one to which these young people orient. They may also find that they can readily recognise 'sounding', but they may feel that it would be an extremely difficult task to specify in any determinate fashion the criteria which enable them, like members, to recognise instances of 'sounding'. Alternatively, these observers might hold the view that to specify the linguistic and contextual criteria would be a possible but pointless task, that to accomplish it effectively would be too time-consuming from the point of view of their overall aims in analysis, and unnecessary in the light of conventions which relate to the reporting of observation work in sociology. These positions avoid the problems raised in this book; and they avoid them in such a way that often no intellectual purchase can be gained on them from such observational work because they are glossed and receive little or no explicit attention. When the issue of description does receive attention it is often covered by some general idea of an inductive process. Schatzman and Strauss write that: 'A researcher will continue shifting his grounds as he creates or changes his classes, until all his prepared classes are displaced by those based upon observation.' (1973, p. 113.)

Presumably *one* basis upon which a class of activity may come to be useful is that the class seems to have some significance for members themselves. But even if our young people appear to orient their talk and behaviour to the notion of a class of behaviour called 'sounding', this leaves outstanding a number of analytic issues. For example, is the identification of someone as 'sounding' similar to formulating an utterance as a command or as 'putting someone down', and if so can we make explicit the way in which contextual features allow us to make such formulations? This will be a level of analysis which will be relevant to much sociology, irrespective of whether one chooses to formulate the problem in ethnomethodological terms. Labelling approaches to the analysis of deviance, for example, must consider the way in which contextual and other features lead to the ascription of labels by authoritative persons; but to say this is simply to state the basis of the descriptive problem which constitutes the theme of this book.

So far I have tried to avoid a discussion of the procedural claims made by ethnomethodologists *vis-à-vis* mainstream sociology, but at the present time any book which did not pay some attention to this issue would be ignoring what for many sociologists are their primary doubts about ethnomethodolgy. I suspect that many sociologists would acknowledge its relevance to micro-issues concerned with language and meaning, but might want to deny any radical claims by ethnomethodologists to reconstitue the foundations of sociological study, along with their characterisation of much that passes for conventional sociological knowledge. These issues have generated a good deal of heat in sociology over the last five years, so it is important to begin by setting out as carefully as possible what the procedural claims of ethnomethodology are *vis-à-vis* present-day sociology.

An important intial point is the difficulty of characterising ethno-methodologists in any unambiguous way, because the extent to which they see some radical distinction between their own work and that of the conventional sociologist diverges widely. Cicourel, for example, is cautious in the claims he makes for ethnomethodology. He writes:

> The observer-researcher must rely upon interpretative procedures when subsuming 'recognised' behavioural displays under concepts derived from his scientific vocabulary. Hence unless the researcher clarifies, conceptually and empirically, his reliance on interpretative procedures, he cannot make claims to 'objective' findings. [1973, pp. 39–40]

Both here, and in his earlier writings, Cicourel's view appears to be that a specification of the interpretative procedures highlighted in ethnomethodological study is a necessary component of any sociological investigation, but that it essentially supplements and puts on a surer footing existing sociological practices – the practices of classification, theory construction and testing, causal inference, and so on. To this extent his views are similar to those of writers like Glaser and Strauss (1967), for whom the rationale for considering members' interpretations of events and inductive classification procedures is that they generate a more valid and powerful conceptual apparatus such that subsequent theoretical work is likely

to be more successful. At the other extreme we have writers like
Blum and McHugh who, while accepting the insights and approach
to language offered in the writings of Garfinkel, conclude that this
has radical implications for the activity of doing sociology. If
members' formulations of scenes and behaviour are problematic, in
the way I indicated in Chapter 4 then surely, they argue, an analyst's
formulations of hearings and machinery are also problematic, susceptible to the same kind of scrutiny which ethnomethodologists
give to a member's talk. They write that:

> To write is to forget why you write; to be caught up in the
> activity of formulation is to face away from one's own funda-
> mental grounds through which those formulations come about . . .
> Since we treat every finding, every speech, every chapter in this
> book as mere surface reflection of what makes them possible,
> since no speech is in this sense perfect or self-sufficient, speaking
> and writing is always from the perspective of analysis an
> inadequate activity. In being done it always makes available for
> analysis a new problem, namely how *it* is possible.
> [McHugh et al, 1974, p. 3]

For this group the only kind of general knowledge is that which
emerges from the process in which speakers/writers continually
explore the grounds on which their formulations are arrived at in
relation to the topic at hand, so that articles written by members of
the group are *essentially* unfinished, and the process of responding
to and exploring each other's research papers comes to be an
integral part of the research strategy. Criteria of adequacy, of
success or failure in analysis, become unclear and aribitrary, since
any particular presentation is always open to further modification.
In fact, readers are urged to participate in such modification (ibid.,
p. 10). The grounds upon which a group of writers cease to col-
laborate on a theme, and decide that it is time to put their ideas into
print are unclear, and all that the person who synthesises the results
of collaboration can do is to provide the reader with some idea of
the dynamic interplay of ideas which has occurred among the
collaborators.

   The group of ethnomethodologists dealt with most extensively in
this book take up a position somewhere between those just outlined.
On the one hand, they see an irreconcilable difference of interests
between themselves and what they call 'constructive' sociological
analysis, but on the other they see it as being possible to pursue

those forms of knowledge which they consider more pertinent in the context of explicit criteria of adequacy, so that the obvious epistemological problems of Blum and McHugh are avoided. Conventional sociology is viewed as 'constructive' in that its various procedures operate with data taken to constitute correct descriptions of scenes, persons, institutions or whatever. But Garfinkel's argument is that to formulate a description (say of an utterance) is always to *select* a description of that utterance, and that selection is an accomplishment (a construction), the nature of which becomes the topic of enquiry for ethnomethodology. Insofar as conventional sociology purports to deal with correct descriptions, then sociologists are selecting descriptions, and their methods of reading utterances and seeing scenes become the data for ethnomethodological study, just as the methods which other people make use of to get the sense of paintings, talk, scenes, people's personality, and so on, become data for study. Essentially ethnomethodology is indifferent to the findings of constructive sociology; it brackets the products of such investigation and chooses instead to pursue and answer a different set of questions.

At the same time, critical sources of tension necessarily appear between the two strategies, since the premises of the ethnomethodological approach derive directly from a critique of what are taken to be the ground rules of sociological analysis. Conventional sociologists are taken to suppose that in specific instances they can arrive at an independent, objective description of what is going on, but Garfinkel is at pains to stress that in any given instance this is always uncertain: '. . . wherever practical actions are topics of study the promised distinction and substitutability of objective for indexical expressions remains programmatic in every *particular* case and on every *actual* occasion in which the distinction or substitutability must be demonstrated.' (1967, p. 6, his emphases.) His stress on specific instances and actual occasions is an important one, because some sociologists may feel that they would not want to make these sorts of claims, in specific instances. They may feel that the criteria which ethnomethodologists demand for an adequate description are too demanding in some way, and that when ethnomethodologists criticise them for not living up to such criteria they are, in effect, tilting at a straw man. Consequently, the descriptive categories employed in their generalisations have a different and distinct status from that attributed to them by ethnomethodologists, a status defined according to the prevailing and available research technology which allows systematic statements about society to be made. Thus some sociologists criticise ethnomethodologists for being more positivistic than most sociologists in their demands for rigorous and literal description as a necessary condition for an adequate constructivist sociology.

There is clearly much in these arguments. One of my themes in this book has been that sociological researchers have explicitly and implicitly drawn back from claiming that they can retrieve descriptions of events and utterances according to a set of fixed criteria, so that when Garfinkel suggests that there are irremediable problems in arriving at objective descriptions of practical actions in any instance, his claim is unlikely to fall on deaf ears. One contribution of ethnomethodology, nevertheless, has been to specify the nature of the problems involved here as being bound up with language and the ways in which we use language. This does not just pose problems for sociologists, it also poses problems for members of a society, so that rules and claims which members make are always liable to be undercut, disputed, contradicted and faulted by virtue of the looseness in the way in which language is used. Yet as we have seen, the models of men and interaction constructed in conventional sociology have done scant justice to these phenomena which litter our everyday lives and are such an integral part of the world we live in. If it is accepted that in any instance sociological descriptions (like those of Sudnow cited in Chapter 1) can be undercut in much the same way that those of members can, then the precise status of constructive sociological knowledge becomes unclear, and the main import of ethnomethodology for sociologists is to raise anew questions concerning the status of their knowledge.

Goldthorpe (1973) has argued forcefully that on this matter sociologists should at least be ontologically pluralistic and recognise that there are different kinds of knowledge about society, each of which can be adequately studied at its own level of analysis.[6] Aspects of the social world come to have a reality *sui generis*, he argues, so that phenomena such as laws, regulations, customary practices, points of etiquette, linguistic forms and so on can become objects of analysis in their own right. In one sense they can be viewed and studied as phenomena which are interpreted in interaction, but they are not just symbolic expressions of people's mental states or invocable features of interaction, and they merit some form of distinctive analysis. I find myself in agreement with these arguments, but I also suspect that few ethnomethodologists would want to make strong claims against them. Clearly laws, rules, etiquette and so on are more than mentalistic constructs and do, in some sense, exist independently of situations of their use. Clearly, there is also room for a sociology which gives us information about the prevailing laws, rules, customs and so on extant in a particular society. On these grounds I find Sudnow's discussion of plea bargaining, referred to in Chapter 1, informative in that it tells me something about the conventions and procedures operating in the setting which he studies. In fact if conventions did not, in some sense, exist independently of particular occasions of use, it is difficult to see how the kind of analysis undertaken by Turner (described in Chapter 3), with the machinery of permissibles and responsibles, would be at all possible.

However, Goldthorpe wants to claim more than this. Those macro-features which have a reality *sui generis*, he argues, also act as conditions of action and can constrain that action. Furthermore, they may do so without participants themselves being aware of this, so that they can produce consequences in action which are unintended on the part of participants. It is in this area of the interaction between conventions and ongoing conduct that ethnomethodological work has most bearing. Take the example of a linguistic form, which Goldthorpe cites as an example of a reality *sui generis*, (ibid., p. 456). A problem which I have examined in this book is whether attempts to extract the distinctive features of such linguistic forms do provide us with information which allows us to demonstrate that the meaning attached to a token of this form is provided for by the distinctive features. My conclusion is that the information given in such attempts does not allow us to attach meaning to expressions in any adequate way. Furthermore, the way in which the distinctive features of a linguistic form constrain the meaning attached to a token in an instance cannot be provided for in any general way, according to a set of rules, or whatever. Similarly with speech acts such as promising. To argue that in our society promising has some central features which constrain interaction in any instance, one must set up such general features and demonstrate in any instance precisely where and how this constraint operates. To do this involves deciding in each case whether or not a promise has been made, but I have argued that from analytic viewpoint this is always ambiguous, that alternative formulations are always available and often in fact made use of by members themselves in their attempts to justify, excuse, defend, fault and so on. To claim that conventions such as those surrounding etiquette have unintended consequences for human conduct, requires the analyst to interpret and describe a person's actions as an instance of a

D*

strategy or a rule of which the actor is unaware; but again, in any instance, alternative formulations of other analysts and, in this case, members themselves, will always be available so that fundamental descriptive problems remain.[7]

The problem of alternative formulations, which is tied for ethno-methodologists to the nature and use of language, is clearly at the heart of some of these issues and, as I have tried to stress, it is a problem only if one sees as a significant and problematic issue the ability of the sociologist in any instance to ascertain the meaning of utterances for participants. To some extent conventional socio-logists do recognise this as a problem in that writers like Goldthorpe are prepared to acknowledge that it cannot be made an unprob-lematic assumption in *all* cases. What he rejects is the view that '. . . in all situations alike an assumption of basic consensus on meanings and definitions will be equally inappropriate' (op. cit., p. 454) and he prefers to think of this matter as an empirical question which is only decidable on a case-by-case basis. He is, of course, right insofar as this is probably the way many sociologists do think of such matters, and insofar as they rely on various reliability measures in order to ensure that there is some kind of measured consensus as to the application of their descriptive categories. I also think that he is right in suggesting that the issue is not one which can be resolved by assumption, that it is an empirical ques-tion. That is why, in the course of this book, I have tried to tackle the question empirically wherever possible, though my own con-clusions would be different, since I think that, for certain analytic purposes, there is a strong case to be made that the substitution of objective for indexical expressions is problematic in any instance. From this premise, which the arguments of writers like Goldthorpe do not seriously question, the ethnomethodologists develop a dis-tinctive research strategy for the analysis of talk and interaction.

My argument then, is, that the ethnomethodologists are in-different to the findings and procedures of constructive sociology, and that in principle, though rarely in practice, these procedures would only be interesting as a topic for ethnomethodological enquiry. The radical implications of ethnomethodology for constructive sociology depend a good deal on the aims and proposals of the latter. For example, Goldthorpe writes that:

> . . . when sociologists place the results of their enquiries and their explanations in competition with members' accounts and seek to 'remedy' these, the basis on which they may properly do so is not

primarily . . . a claim to greater objectivity and freedom from bias. It is, rather, that they are able in this way to open up possibilities for discussion of a better grounded and more consequential character.

[op. cit., p. 451]

If the aims of a constructive sociology are simply to open up various grounds for discussion, if they are simply to promote rational discussion of the laws, customs and mores which *do* exist and which, in some sense, guide our conduct, then there can surely be little friction between the two approaches. Once stronger claims are made – claims, for example, that in this instance behaviour is a product of norms – then the ethnomethodological critique becomes a telling one and one which, I hope, will lead to a careful assessment of the status of the knowledge being employed in constructive sociology.

Notes

CHAPTER 1

1 I should stress that the specific studies selected for close discussion in this book have been chosen on the grounds that they are not fringe or marginal studies, but studies which have made an important contribution to their field and which many students interested in language will probably have come across. In short, I have selected them because I find their arguments challenging and worthy of close scrutiny. More specifically, as regards the Sudnow article, it should be mentioned that Sudnow's research strategies in relation to language analysis have changed fairly radically since this article was published. See, for example, his article 'Temporal parameters of interpersonal observation' in D. Sudnow ed. (1972).

2 For British readers the District Attorney is roughly equivalent to our prosecuting counsel, the Public Defender to our defence counsel.

3 This notion will be elaborated more fully in later chapters, especially Chapter 4.

4 This, of course, is only an *emphasis*. Lyons, for example, in an introduction to theoretical linguistics, still sees fit to include a fairly extensive discussion of reference. (See Lyons, 1968, Section 9.4.)

5 Other semantic markers such as (Animate) (Living) and (Physical Object) are also, of course, relevant to the meaning of the word 'bachelor', but the number of entries, it is argued, can be reduced by redundancy rules. These rules add semantic markers to lexical items when such markers are completely predictable from other semantic markers already assigned to that item. The distinction between distinguishers and semantic markers has come in for a good deal of linguistic criticism, and for a more recent formulation of the Fodor/ Katz type of approach see Katz (1972).

6 For a relatively brief and clear overview of developments in linguistic semantics see Maclay (1971).

7 For a good historical overview of philosophical semantics see Kretzmann (1967). His coverage of twentieth-century developments, however, is very thin.

8 Ryle (1963) points out that different arguments would also be consistent with Mill's writing; these differences will not be touched on here.

9 This argument is derived from Chapter 1 of Alston (1964).

10 This extract is quoted in Pitkin (Chapter 2, 1972), who also provides a straightforward account of Wittgenstein's views on ostensive definition. Further valuable discussion is contained in Cavell (1961–2).

11 A book edited by Lyas (1971, Part 3) contains several articles by philosophers and linguists in which such matters are debated.

CHAPTER 2

1 This chapter will not pay much explicit attention to the relationship

between linguistic and cognitive categories. The literature pertaining to this does not ameliorate the kinds of difficulties which I find with componential analysis, and a discussion of this issue is outside the scope of this short book. For a good introduction to the relevant arguments see Section 4 of Tyler (1969). This book of readings also provides the best single source of anthropological work in the field of componential analysis which is known to me. There are several good introductions to componential analysis from both the linguistic and anthropological points of view. In the former category I would suggest Lyons (1968, Chapter 10), Bierwisch (1970), Leech (1974, Chapter 6), Lehrer (1974, Chapters 2–3). In the latter, Tyler (1969, Introduction), Frake (1962) and Burling (1970, Chapters 1–6).

2   See Goodenough (1965). For a critique of this work see Schneider (1965). Both these articles are reprinted in Tyler (1969).

3   Frake does not provide us with any numerical weight for this consensus, but one of his main arguments is that while there is consensus about the relevance of particular criterial features to diagnoses in abstract discussion of diseases, in practice, when confronted with having to make a diagnosis, there is nevertheless a good deal of argument concerning the correct diagnosis (see especially 1961, p. 130).

4   All the examples below are taken from Leech (1974, Chapter 6). The scope, methods and possibilities of this technique in linguistics are only touched on here, and readers who wish to explore this in more detail could begin by following up the appropriate references in Note 1.

5   I should stress that in this argument I am glossing over an important distinction between what Frake calls 'distinctive semantic features' and 'criterial features'. Distinctive semantic features, he argues, are a result of matching a word used to the perceptual or analytic attributes of what it denotes. In describing the distinctive semantic features of a colour term, for example, one has an independent measure, an etic grid, along which the range of application of a given colour term can be plotted (see Berlin and Kay, 1970). Frake stresses that his own 'criterial features' of diagnoses are not derived in this way, but on the basis of the ways in which Subanun themselves distinguish verbally between the bases for different diagnoses (see especially 1961, pp. 122–3).

6   See, for example, the proceedings of the 'Public Inquiry into the Acts of Violence and Civil Disorders in Northern Ireland', (the 'Scarman Tribunal'), 1969, Day No. 3, where the Chairman agrees with the Prime Minister of Northern Ireland that the Tribunal seeks '. . . to determine precisely what took place, who began this violence, who introduced the use of firearms into an already grave situation, who was responsible for the extensive damage, the injuries and the loss of life' (p. 2).

7   This term is taken from Hart (1951, p. 148) who uses it to emphasise that legal concepts such as 'contract' cannot in any strict sense be provided for by a set of necessary and sufficient conditions, that these conditions are always subject to being modified and defeated by further conditions in any specific case. Thus Hart notes that in a case of contract a defence that the defendant has been deceived by misrepresentation on the part of the plaintiff entitles the defendant, in certain cases, to say that the contract is not valid. Much of this article

by Hart is relevant to the themes discussed in this chapter, and his work has influenced certain strands of ethnomethodological writing.

8 For a discussion of these issues see Lehrer (1974).
9 Some of these problems are recognised by Frake himself, and his own critical and perceptive descriptions of particular diagnoses are features which give his work special interest.
10 This is a point also made by Wieder in his discussion of Frake's study (1971, p. 129). Wieder's article makes several relevant points concerning componential analysis and could usefully be read in conjunction with this chapter.
11 The example is taken from Bierwisch (1970, p. 167).
12 I should emphasise that my discussion of componential analysis has not incorporated all sociological discussion of this approach. Habermas (1970), for example, has taken issue with Bierwisch's contention that any universal components of meaning are necessarily produced by the limitations of human beings' sense organs, nervous system and so on. Some of the evidence relevant to this argument is reviewed by Habermas, but the issues are complex and the relevant evidence often inconclusive. For an empirically based discussion of some of these questions in the context of children's first word meanings, the reader could consult Clark (1973).

CHAPTER 3

1 Both Ervin-Tripp and Friedrich stress that there is a good deal of situational variation which the diagram would not account for, and I shall stress the importance of this in my argument. Even allowing for this, Fig. 3.1 seems to omit consideration of certain structural patterns which Friedrich emphasises in his analysis. For example he suggests that there would have been less formality in the mother–daughter relationship, whereas Fig. 3.1 predicts that a daughter would use (V) to her mother (see Friedrich, 1966, p. 234).
2 On this point see Lyons (1968, Chapter 9, Section 3).
3 Grice distinguishes 'meaning *nn*' (i.e. non-natural meaning) from such senses of 'mean' as occur in 'Clouds mean rain' or 'Those spots mean measles'.
4 Similar, but far less explicit, arguments have been developed by Habermas (1970).
5 This rule is slightly re-worded from the original. It also marks a certain divergence of Searle from the approach of Grice in that Searle is concerned to stress the way in which the locutionary meaning of an utterance can limit its illocutionary force and thus influence the nature of the speech act in question. On this point see Searle (1969, pp. 42–50).
6 I want to stress that Searle's aim in pursuing this kind of analysis is not to provide a set of conditions which will allow an analyst to distinguish in a text real promises from defective ones. From Searle's point of view, his analysis bears most strongly on his philosophical aim of deriving 'ought' statements from 'is' statements, and readers interested in this dimension of Searle's work could look at Part 3 of W. Hudson ed. (1969) for a statement of the philosophical debates which his work has stirred up. Nevertheless, it does seem to me relevant and legitimate to examine whether, and in what sense, such conditions

can be fulfilled, and insofar as Searle's arguments rely on such empirical possibilities, our discussion may have some bearing on his overall thesis.

7 Similar arguments could be developed in relation to other conditions for promising cited by Searle, especially conditions (v) and (vii), but their elaboration in this context would become burdensome.

CHAPTER 4

1 There are a number of general statements of the ethnomethodological position. Among the best are Garfinkel (1967), Garfinkel and Sacks (1970), Zimmerman and Pollner (1971). Much can be learnt from debates between ethnomethodologists and their critics. See, for example, Denzin (1971) and Zimmerman and Wieder (1971); or Taylor, Walton and Young (1973, pp. 192–208) and Coulter (1974).

2 This example is adapted from Garfinkel and Sacks (1970, p. 350) whose paper contains extensive discussion of formulations. The interview between I and B is not drawn from this article, however, and is my own artificial concoction.

3 His book *Studies in Ethnomethodology* (1967) is the source of the material I use here.

4 It is possible to see a false dichotomy in this quotation, but Garfinkel does not want to suggest that shared conventional knowledge constitutes an insignificant dimension of any inquiry. We shall see later that such knowledge is invoked by ethnomethodologists, but their primary task is the discovery of members' common *methods* of arriving at the sense of events. This, as I understand it, is the sense in which the extract needs to be read.

5 It should be emphasised that 'context' here includes, as always, the knowledge which each participant in a conversational exchange has of other members.

6 The conversation below was taken by Turner from Pittenger, Hockett and Danehy (1960).

7 As Turner's article is still in press, page numbers refer to pages in the manuscript copy. It may seem perverse to take an unpublished article at this point, but this paper stands as a good example of ethnomethodological work and a variety of points can be readily illustrated from it.

8 Turner also provides us with some machinery for hearing this utterance as a complaint.

9 Turner does not attempt to condense and formalise his analysis in the way in which I do below. For this reason the set of machinery below is better thought of as a summary of Turner's argument than a formal statement of the machinery. In my subsequent discussion, however, I shall refer to it as a machinery.

10 One could also, of course, diminish a complaint by noticing that f is not a member of the class of responsibles for such activities. Thus the psychiatrist could have said something which was heard as 'Your husband's surely not a tyrant.' In *this* machinery, however, we do not need to consider this, as Turner's concern is only to provide for the hearing 'Surely you're old enough to be responsible for your own decisions.'

11 These claims are made most explicitly in the later part of his article, especially p. 30 onwards.

12 This example is taken from a paper by Stubbs (1973).

13 It is important to stress, however, that the phenomena of misunderstanding and breakdowns in 'shared meaning' become susceptible to analysis within the framework of ethnomethodology, whereas such features have received little attention from other theoretical traditions within sociology, such as symbolic interactionism.

14 Schegloff and Sacks' position on this issue is not necessarily inconsistent with the premises of the ethnomethodological strategy, so long as they do not claim that in any stretch of talk members can *only* be heard as orienting to the machinery which they provide.

15 A second group of ethnomethodologists centres round Cicourel, and readers interested in the intellectual position of this group could begin by looking at Cicourel (1968, 1973).

CHAPTER 5

1 A relatively recent, clear and illuminating exposition of his theoretical views on these issues is contained in Bernstein (1971, Chapter 8).

2 It is a major shortcoming of the literature on children that little systematic attention has been paid to the naturally occurring interaction problems which they find themselves involved in with adults, and the strategies they develop to cope with these problems. One or two articles make a start in this direction, such as Wood, Weinstein and Parker (1967) and Dubin and Dubin (1963).

3 I do not want to suggest that this utterance, and the others referred to in the following section, can only be heard in one way. I am simply using these examples to highlight how the meaning of utterances in the context of parent–child speech is not given by the formal structure of the utterance (e.g. its structure as an imperative or a question).

4 Cook-Gumperz, in Appendix 1 of her study (1973), gives a fairly detailed account of the procedures used to ensure high levels of agreement among coders. It does not provide us with the sort of evidence which might allow us to illustrate the above processes in any detail, but it is a particularly frank and useful account of coding procedures.

5 There are, of course, various further ways in which the problematic nature of coding procedures can be concealed. For example, in my own study concerning children's speech (1974) I find myself citing as examples of the coding categories (and as examples in the text) those which appear to be less problematic than many others as regards their classification.

6 The discussion of Labov's work in Chapter 3 is directly relevant to the discussion here, since it is specifically concerned with commands.

7 The following notational conventions are necessary to understand Fig. 1:

$a \rightarrow \begin{bmatrix} x \\ y \end{bmatrix}$ = there is a system x/y with entry condition a; if a, then either x or y

$a \begin{cases} \rightarrow \begin{bmatrix} x \\ y \end{bmatrix} \\ \rightarrow \begin{bmatrix} m \\ n \end{bmatrix} \end{cases}$ = There are 2 simultaneous systems x/y and m/n; both have entry condition a; if a, then both either x or y and, independently, either m or n

I should emphasise that Turner's discussion contains full meaning potential analyses for commands, threats, disapprobation and reparation-seeking, all of which are excluded here for our purposes. The kinds of formal linguistic description used need not concern us here.

8 Clearly the *first* decision is to classify an utterance as an instance of imperative control or positional control, and the selection between commands, threats etc, is determined to some extent by this prior selection. This does not affect my argument materially, however.

9 One way out of such predicaments is to see speech as multi-functional, and classify accordingly. This is not very satisfactory since it can involve classifying any individual utterance as an instance of a variety of quite different speech acts. While it is a logical recognition of these problems, it resolves them in an unsatisfactory way, since in effect it claims that utterances are *heard* as multi-functional, whereas hearers (children in the example I am dealing with here) probably do not hear speech in this way.

10 See, for example, C. Taylor (1964).

11 See, for example, Peters (1958): 'A motive is not necessarily a discreditable reason for acting, but it is a reason asked for in a context where there is a suggestion that it *might* be discreditable. The demand is for justification, not simply explanation' (p. 31). I imagine that it is for this reason that sociologists who have worked in this field since Wright Mills have tended to see it as part and parcel of deviance analysis.

12 For a discussion of these matters see Hart (1968), Chapter 4.

13 I want to make clear that in his article Taylor does *not* in fact claim that the magistrate's ratings can be related in any clearcut way to specific judgements which they make. The points made here are not so much a criticism of his claims as a consideration of the status of his data.

14 Blum and McHugh have published an article (1971) which gives some idea of what an ethnomethodological approach to the analysis of motives would look like. However, they sharply distinguish their own enterprise from that of ethnomethodology. For example, they write, 'Whereas ethnomethodology uses the ordinary world "seriously" [they hope to solve analytic problems by doing naturalistic science on this world], we treat the everyday world as a proximate occasion for initiating inquiry and not as a "fact" to be reproduced' (p. 99).

CHAPTER 6

1 See Martins (1974), p. 251.

2 I am thinking particularly here of Winch (1958) and Louch (1966).

3 See Lassman (1974), p. 128. Lassman's characterisation of ethnomethodology as sharing these consensual biases however seems to me misplaced (see op. cit., p. 141). In fact, one of the notable features of ethnomethodology is that it can make discontinuities in meaning a topic for explicit analysis.

4 For a more extensive discussion of these issues see Zimmerman and Wieder (1971).

5 For a preliminary survey and careful discussion of some of these findings see Brown (1973), pp. 32–51.

6 Goldthorpe's review article seems to me one of the more informed general appraisals of ethnomethodology to have appeared in recent years, though it suffers particularly from a misplaced emphasis on the writing of Douglas rather than, say, the more authoritative work of Garfinkel, an inadequate consideration of the distinctive research strategy adopted by ethnomethodology, and a misconstruction of the approach as being essentially idealist in the traditional sense.

7 This is the kind of problem which persists unacknowledged in Goffman's various writings and sharply differentiates his work from that of the ethnomethodologists.

Bibliography

Alston, W. P., *Philosophy of Language* (New Jersey, Prentice-Hall, 1964).

Ariel, S., 'Semantic Tests', *Man*, Vol. 11 (1967), pp. 535–50.

Austin, J. L., *Philosophical Papers* (Oxford, Clarendon Press, 1961).
How to Do Things with Words (Oxford, Clarendon Press, 1962).

Bambrough, R., 'Universals and Family Resemblances', pp. 186–205 of Pitcher, G., ed., *Wittgenstein* (London, Macmillan, 1966).

Barker, R. and Wright, H., *Midwest and its Children* (New York, Row, Peterson, 1955).

Bendix, E. H., 'Componential Analysis of General Vocabulary', *International Journal of American Linguistics*, Vol. 32 (1966), Supplements.

Berlin, B. and Kay, P., *Basic Colour Terms* (Berkeley, University of California Press, 1970).

Bernstein, B., ed., *Class, Codes and Control*, Vol. 1 (London, Routledge & Kegan Paul, 1971).

Bierwisch, M., 'Semantics' Chapter 8, in Lyons, J., ed., *New Horizons in Linguistics* (Harmondsworth, Penguin, 1970).

Blom, J-P. and Gumperz, J., 'Social meaning in linguistic structure: code switching in Norway', in Gumperz, J. and Hymes, D., eds, *Directions in Sociolinguistics* (New York, Holt, Rinehart & Winston, 1972).

Bloomfield, L., *Language* (New York, Holt, 1933).

Blum, A. F. and McHugh, P., 'The Social Ascription of Motives', *American Sociological Review*, Vol. 36 (1971), pp. 98–109.

Brittan, A., *Meanings and Situations* (London, Routledge & Kegan Paul, 1973).

Brown, R., *A First Language* (London, Allen & Unwin, 1973).

Brown, R. and Ford, M., 'Address in American English', pp. 234–45 of Hymes, D., ed. (1964).

Burling, R., *Man's Many Voices* (New York, Holt, Rinehart & Winston, 1970).

Carroll, J. B., ed., *Language, Thought and Reality: Selected Writings of B. L. Whorf* (Cambridge (Mass.), M.I.T. Press, 1956).

Caton, C. E., 'Overview', pp. 3–14 of Steinberg, D. D. and Jakobovits, L. A., eds (1971).

Cavell, S., 'The Claim to Rationality' Unpublished Ph.D. dissertation, Harvard University (1961–2).

Chomsky, N., *Syntactic Structures* (The Hague, Mouton, 1957).

Aspects of the Theory of Syntax (Cambridge (Mass.), M.I.T. Press, 1965).

Cicourel, A. V., *The Social Organization of Juvenile Justice* (New York, Wiley, 1968).

Cognitive Sociology (Harmondsworth, Penguin, 1973).

Clark, E. V., 'What's in a Word? On the Child's Acquisition of Semantics in his First Language', pp. 65–110 of Moore, T. E. ed., *Cognitive Development and the Acquisition of Language* (Academic Press, New York, 1973).

Conklin, H. C., 'Hanunóo Colour Categories', *Southwestern Journal of Anthropology*, Vol. II (1955), pp. 339–44.

'Ethnogenealogical Method', in Goodenough, W. H., ed., *Explorations in Cultural Anthropology* (New York, McGraw-Hill, 1964).

Cook-Gumperz, J., *Social Control and Socialization* (London, Routledge & Kegan Paul, 1973).

Coulter, J., 'Language and the Conceptualization of Meaning', *Sociology*, Vol. 7, No. 2 (1973).

'What's Wrong with the New Criminology', *Sociological Review*, Vol. 22 (1974), pp. 119–35.

Denzin, N. K., 'Symbolic Interactionism and Ethnomethodology', pp. 259–85 of Douglas, J. D., ed. (1971).

Douglas, J. D., ed., *Understanding Everyday Life* (London, Routledge & Kegan Paul, 1971).

Dubin, E. R. and Dubin, R., 'The Authority Inception Period in Socialization', *Child Development*, Vol. 34 (1963), pp. 885–98.

Ervin-Tripp, S. M., 'Sociolinguistics', pp. 15–92 of Fishman, J. A., ed., *Advances in the Sociology of Language*, Vol. 1 (The Hague, Mouton, 1971).

Fillmore, C. J., 'Types of Lexical Information', pp. 370–93 of Steinberg, D. D. and Jakobovits, L. A., eds (1971).

Fodor, J. and Katz, J., *The Structure of Language* (New Jersey, Prentice-Hall, 1964).

Frake, C. O., 'The ethnographic study of cognitive systems' in Gladwin, T. and Sturtevant, W. C., eds, *Anthropology and Human Behaviour* (Washington, Anthropological Society of Washington, 1962).

'The Diagnosis of Disease Among the Subanun of Mindinao', *American Anthropologist*, Vol. 63, No. 1 (1961).

Friedrich, P., 'Structural Implications of Russian Pronominal Usage', pp. 214–53 of Bright, W., ed., *Sociolinguistics* (The Hague, Mouton, 1966).

Garfinkel, H., *Studies in Ethnomethodology* (New Jersey, Prentice-Hall, 1967).

Garfinkel, H. and Sacks, H., 'On Formal Structures of Practical Actions', pp. 338–66 of McKinney, J. C. and Tiryakian, E. A., eds, *Theoretical Sociology* (New York, Appleton-Century-Crofts, 1970).

Gerth, H. and Mills, C. W., *Character and Social Structure* (London, Routledge & Kegan Paul, 1954).

Glaser, B. G. and Strauss, A., *The Discovery of Grounded Theory* (Chicago, University of Chicago Press, 1967).

Goffman, E., 'On Cooling the Mark Out: Some Aspects of Adaptation to Failure', pp. 482–505 of Rose, A., ed. (1962).

Goldthorpe, J., 'A Revolution in Sociology?' (review article), *Sociology*, Vol. 7 (1973), pp. 449–62.

Goodenough, W. H., 'Yankee Kinship Terminology', *American Anthropologist*, Vol. 67 (1965), pp. 259–87.

Grice, P., 'Meaning', *Philosophical Review*, (July 1957), pp. 377–88.

Habermas, J., 'Towards a Theory of Communicative Competence', *Inquiry*, Vol. 13, (1970), pp. 360–75.

Hart, H. L. A., 'The Ascription of Responsibility and Rights', Chapter 8 of Flew, A., ed., *Logic and Language* (Oxford, Blackwell, 1951).
Punishment and Responsibility (Oxford, Clarendon Press, 1968).

Hartung, F. E., *Crime, Law and Society* (Detroit, Wayne State University Press, 1965).

Householder, F. W., *Linguistic Speculations* (Cambridge, Cambridge University Press, 1971).

Hudson, W. D., ed., *The Is–Ought Question* (London, Macmillan, 1969).

Hymes, D., 'The Ethnography of Speaking', pp. 13–53 of Gladwin, T. and Sturtevant, W. C., eds, *Anthropology and Human Behaviour* (Washington, Anthropological Society of Washington, 1962).

Hymes, D., ed., *Language in Culture and Society* (New York, Harper & Row, 1964).

Katz, J., *Semantic Theory* (New York, Harper & Row, 1972).

Kretzmann, N., 'Semantics, History of' in Edwards, P., ed., *Encyclopaedia of Philosophy*, Vol. 7 (1967).

Labov, W., *The Social Stratification of English in New York City* (Washington, Centre for Applied Linguistics, 1966).
'Rules for Ritual Insults', pp. 120–69 of Sudnow, D., ed. (1972).

Lassman, P., 'Phenomenological Perspectives in Sociology', pp. 125–45 of Rex, J., ed. (1974).

Leech, G., *Semantics* (Harmondsworth, Penguin Books, 1974).

Lehrer, A., *Semantic Fields and Lexical Structure* (Amsterdam, North Holland Publishing Co., 1974).

Louch, A. R., *Explanation and Human Action* (Oxford, Blackwell, 1966).

Lyas, C., ed., *Philosophy and Linguistics* (London, Macmillan, 1971).

Lyons, J., *Introduction to Theoretical Linguistics* (Cambridge, Cambridge University Press, 1968).

Maclay, H., 'Overview', pp. 157–82 of Steinberg, D. D. and Jakobovits, L. A., eds (1971).

McHugh, P., Raffel, S., Foss, D. C. and Blum, A. F., *On the Beginning of Social Inquiry* (London, Routledge & Kegan Paul, 1974).

Martins, H., 'Time and Theory in Sociology', pp. 246–94 of Rex, J., ed. (1974).

Mead, G. H., *Mind, Self and Society* (Chicago, University of Chicago Press, 1967).

Mill, J. S., *System of Logic*, Books I and IV (1843, many editions).

Perchonock, N. and Werner, O., 'Navaho Systems of Classification and Some Implications for Ethnoscience', *Ethnology*, Vol. 8 (1969), pp. 229–43.

Peters, R. S., *The Concept of Motivation* (London, Routledge & Kegan Paul, 1958).

Pitkin, H. F., *Wittgenstein and Justice* (Berkeley, University of California Press, 1972).

Pittenger, R., Hockett, C. F. and Danehy, J. J., *The First Five Minutes* (New York, Paul Martineau, 1960).

Proceedings of the Public Inquiry Into the Acts of Violence and Civil Disorders in Northern Ireland (HMSO, 1969).

Rex, J., ed., *Approaches to Sociology* (London, Routledge & Kegan Paul, 1974).

Rose, A., ed., *Human Behaviour and Social Processes* (London, Routledge & Kegan Paul, 1962).

Rushing, W. A., *The Psychiatric Professions* (Chapel Hill, University of North Carolina Press, 1964).

Ryle, G., 'The Theory of Meaning', pp. 128–53 of Caton, C. E., ed., *Philosophy and Ordinary Language* (Urbana, University of Illinois Press, 1963).

Sacks, H., Mimeographed lecture notes, (17 April 1968).

Sacks, H., Jefferson, G. and Schegloff, E., 'A Simplest Systematics for the Organization of Turn Taking in Conversation', *Language* (forthcoming).

Saussure, F. de *Cours de Linguistique Générale* (Paris, Payot, 1916).

Schatzman, L. and Strauss, A., *Field Research* (New Jersey, Prentice-Hall, 1973).

Schegloff, E. A., 'Notes on a Conversational Practice: Formulating Place', pp. 95–135 of Giglioli, P. P., ed., *Language and Social Context* (Harmonsworth, Penguin, 1972).

Schegloff, E. A. and Sacks, H., 'Opening Up Closings', *Semiotica*, Vol. 8 (1973), pp. 289–327.

Schneider, D., 'American Kin Terms and Terms for Kinsmen', *American Anthropologist*, Vol. 67 (1965), pp. 288–308.

Schutz, A., *Collected Papers* Vol. 1 (The Hague, M. Nijhoff, 1967).

Scott, M. and Lyman, S., 'Accounts', *American Sociological Review*, Vol. 33, No. 1 (1968).

Searle, J., *Speech Acts* (Cambridge, Cambridge University Press, 1969).

Stanton, A. H. and Schwartz, M. S., *The Mental Hospital* (New York, Basic Books, 1954).

Steinberg, D. D. and Jakobovits, L. A., eds, *Semantics* (Cambridge, Cambridge University Press, 1971).

Strauss, A. et al, 'The Hospital and its Negotiated Order', pp. 147–69 of Friedson, E., ed., *The Hospital in Modern Society* (New York, The Free Press, 1963).

Strawson, P. F., 'Intention and Convention in Speech Acts', *Philosophical Review*, (October 1964), pp. 439–60.

Stubbs, M., 'Some Structural Complexities of Talk in Meetings', Working Paper in Discourse Analysis No. 5 (University of Birmingham, 1973).

Sudnow, D., 'Normal Crimes: Sociological Features of the Penal Code in a Public Defender Office', *Social Problems*, Vol. 12 (1965), pp. 255–76.

Sudnow, D., ed., *Studies in Social Interaction* (New York, The Free Press, 1972).

Taylor, C., *The Explanation of Behaviour* (London, Routledge & Kegan Paul, 1964).

Taylor, I., Walton, P. and Young, J., *The New Criminology* (London, Routledge & Kegan Paul, 1973).

Taylor, L., 'The Significance and Interpretation of Replies to Motivational Questions: the Case of Sex Offenders', *Sociology*, Vol. 6 (1972), pp. 23–39.

Turner, G., 'Social Class and Children's Language of Control at Age Five and Seven', pp. 135–202 of Bernstein, B., ed., *Class, Codes and Control*, Vol. 2 (London, Routledge & Kegan Paul, 1973).

Turner, R., 'Utterance Positioning as an Interactional Resource', in Wilson, R. J., ed., *Ethnomethodology, Labelling Theory and Deviant Behaviour* (London, Routledge & Kegan Paul, forthcoming).

Turner, R. H., 'Role Taking: Process Versus Conformity', pp. 20–41 of Rose, A., ed. (1962).

Tyler, S. A., ed., *Cognitive Anthropology* (New York, Holt, Rinehart & Winston, 1969).

Wieder, D. L., 'On Meaning by Rule', pp. 107–36 of Douglas, J., ed. (1971).

'Telling the Code', pp. 144–73 of Turner, R., ed., *Ethnomethodology* (Harmondsworth, Penguin, 1974).

Winch, P., *The Idea of a Social Science* (London, Routledge & Kegan Paul, 1958).

Wittgenstein, L., *Philosophical Investigations* (Oxford, Blackwell, 1953). *The Blue and Brown Books* (Oxford, Blackwell, 1958).

Wood, J. R., Weinstein, E. A. and Parker, R., 'Children Interpersonal Tactics', *Sociological Inquiry*, Vol. 37 (1967), pp. 129–38.

Wootton, A. J., 'Social class influences on speech patterns in the homes of four-year-old children', Unpublished Ph.D. dissertation (University of Aberdeen, 1972).

'Talk in the Homes of Young Children', *Sociology*, Vol. 8 (1974), pp. 277–95.

Zimmerman, D. and Pollner, M., 'The Everyday World as a Phenomenon', pp. 80–105 of Douglas, J., ed. (1971).

Zimmerman, D. and Wieder, D. L., 'Ethnomethodology and the Problem of Order: Comment on Denzin', pp. 285–99 of Douglas, J., ed. (1971).

Index